THE
URBAN
COMMUNITY

AMERICAN HISTORICAL SOURCES SERIES:
Research and Interpretation

LORMAN RATNER, Editor

PRENTICE-HALL INTERNATIONAL, INC., *London*
PRENTICE-HALL OF AUSTRALIA, PTY. LTD., *Sydney*
PRENTICE-HALL OF CANADA, LTD., *Toronto*
PRENTICE-HALL OF INDIA (PRIVATE) LTD., *New Delhi*
PRENTICE-HALL OF JAPAN, INC., *Tokyo*

Roy Lubove
University of Pittsburgh

THE
URBAN
COMMUNITY

Housing
and Planning
in the
Progressive Era

Prentice-Hall, Inc., Englewood Cliffs, New Jersey

Current printing (last digit):
10   9   8   7   6   5   4   3   2   1

© 1967 by PRENTICE-HALL, INC.
Englewood Cliffs, New Jersey

Library of Congress Catalog Card No.: 67-10119

Printed in the United States of America
C-93916

EDITOR'S FOREWORD

The Urban Community is a volume in the American Historical Sources Series, devoted to the exploration of aspects of American history and to the process of interpreting historical evidence. The introduction to each volume will be followed by some of the key documents used to prepare the essay. Readers are thus invited to share in the experience of turning raw evidence into history. The essays have been written especially for this series, and represent contributions to historical knowledge as well as demonstrations in the writing of history based upon sources included in the work.

Professor Lubove, in this book, discusses phases of urbanization in the progressive era. He invites consideration of some key questions raised by historians studying the late nineteenth and early twentieth centuries. What was the attitude toward cities; toward the role of government, the intellectual and expert; toward public and private responsibility in shaping the urban physical environment? He suggests that historians might profitably devote greater attention to housing, planning, land-use decisions, and related developments which influenced the form and structure of cities. The urbanization process and the problems of environmental and social control it created stimulated the growth of governmental service functions. It led to efforts to enhance the power of social scientists and technicians—in architecture, social work, and other fields. More generally, urbanization was related to many social and political developments of the period, and is therefore central to historical interpretation of progressivism as a whole. Progressivism never died in the sense that we still confront the central issues of urban housing, planning and social organization.

Professor Lubove's discussion of the Regional Planning Association of America bears on another broad issue in current historiography—what happened to progressivism in the 1920's? The work of the RPAA directs attention to important continuities between the 1920's and the reform impulse of the progressive period. Similarly, the experience of the RPAA suggests that important innovations and experiments occurred in the 1920's which have been overlooked because of excessive preoccupation with the 1920's as a period of decline.

This book exemplifies the dual purpose of the American Historical Sources Series: presentation of new views and materials and illumination of the historiographical process.

LORMAN RATNER

CONTENTS

The Roots of Urban Planning

During the late nineteenth and early twentieth centuries, the American city entered a new phase of its history. The long-term demographic revolution, which concentrated a majority of the population in urban areas, was completed by 1920. Americans of the progressive era were thus the first to confront the reality of urban dominance. Many reform efforts of the period—labor legislation, Americanization, prohibition, housing, public health, and good government—were related to problems of city life. More generally, urbanization was synonymous with industrialization and its challenge to traditional institutions. The fact that the progressive era witnessed the definitive transition from a rural to an urban civilization has important implications for the historiography of the period. Potentially, urbanization might serve as a fruitful conceptual framework for interpreting political, economic, and social change.

A substantial body of historical literature on progressivism deals with political events, particularly on the national level. Business developments, including the rise of the corporation, have received considerable attention. In recent years, a number of historians have examined social reform ideologies, welfare organization, and related social issues such as immigration and prohibition. Necessarily, the city often provides the setting for these studies, but a more systematic analysis of the relationship between urbanization and institutional change is needed.

Any such analysis will require that historians devote greater attention to the shaping of the urban physical environment. The city, after all, is basically an artifact, a physical container within which complex

1

human interactions occur; social organization and relationships are greatly influenced by land-use and housing patterns. Prior to the late nineteenth century, urban land and housing were viewed as commodities, subject to the laws of supply and demand. As in the broader economic system, competitive market disciplines presumably guaranteed order and progress. By the late nineteenth century, however, Americans had become less confident that market disciplines would suffice. Planners, housing reformers, and others launched a search for norms of public intervention. They aspired to enlarge the scope of public decision-making. These efforts to institute public controls over land-use and to improve the quality of the housing environment are central to a historiography which adopts urbanization as a conceptual tool. Conservation, housing codes, zoning, city planning, park development, the City Beautiful movement, and the Garden City idea differed in origin, but shared a common objective—an enhanced role for the architect, planner, and welfare expert at the expense of the business interests which had traditionally determined urban land-use policy. The remainder of this essay will be devoted to these movements.

Conservation experts made profound, if indirect, contributions to urban planning. They introduced the concept of scientific, efficient resource utilization. Urban land could be interpreted as one such resource; and urban social reformers frequently adopted the rhetoric of conservation to justify their efforts to improve living and working conditions. They spoke in terms of the need to "conserve" human resources often wasted or exploited in a complex industrial society. Conservation leaders such as John Wesley Powell, Elwood Mead, and Benton MacKaye moved beyond resource policy into the realm of social and community theory. Linking up with the "country life" and "back-to-the-land" movements, these men sought to coordinate new land use and rural community organization principles. Critical of American pioneer tradition which acquiesced in rapid, speculative disposition of the national domain, conservation leaders proposed a policy of administered land use combined with group settlement and the introduction of cooperative institutions.

The settlement of the Plains and Rocky Mountain Region after the Civil War had dramatized the need for radical changes in the national land system. The familiar rectilinear survey and the Homestead principle of dispersed settlement proved increasingly inappropriate as the frontier reached the 100th meridian, where rainfall averaged less than twenty inches a year. John Wesley Powell, geologist in charge of the United States Geographical and Geological Survey of the Rocky Mountain Region, was among the first to formulate an alternative policy. He emphasized that scientific land classification was imperative in a region containing a limited amount of arable land, dependent upon irrigation. These same circumstances demanded a more flexible formula than the rectangular, 160-acre Homestead allotment. Powell suggested that farms of 80 acres and ranches of 2,560 acres were better suited to the region. To insure equitable and efficient water-use, he proposed the establishment of irrigation and pasturage districts. Each would be controlled by nine or more individuals who would be guaranteed access and title to water. These districts might form the nucleus of rural communities; if settlers grouped their homes "to the greatest possible extent," they would benefit more than in the case of the dispersed homestead from the "local social organizations of civilization." [1]

Powell's emphasis upon the advantages of cooperative institutions and group settlement and his interest in the social implications of contrasting land-use systems represented a major contribution to the American planning tradition. He anticipated subsequent programs of scientific land-use, rural cooperation, and rural community planning. The basic principle of administered land-use, coordinated with social objectives, was as applicable to an urban setting as to a rural setting.

Landscape architects served to some degree as the urban counterpart of Powell and his successors in the conservation field. They exerted a major influence in establishing new criteria for urban form and social welfare. Post-Civil War landscape architects such as Frederick Law Olmsted, H. W. S. Cleveland, and Charles Eliot were genuine radicals who espoused the ideal of an urban-rural continuum, or continuous city-park-garden. In their haste to conquer the wilderness, Americans had come to view the city as a man-made environment which subdued nature, if it did not obliterate it. Landscape architects, heirs to the romantic Gothic revival and the "picturesque" estate plan-

---

[1] John Wesley Powell, *Report on the Lands of the Arid Region of the United States, with a More Detailed Account of the Lands of Utah,* ed. Wallace Stegner (Cambridge, Mass.: Harvard University Press, 1962), p. 34. Originally published March, 1879.

ning of Andrew Jackson Downing, evolved a new conception of urban form the long-range significance of which cannot be exaggerated. Their ideal was the community which "would combine the advantages of both town and country" and would "so alternate open spaces with areas occupied by dwellings that it would practically occupy one vast garden." [2]

This community norm resulted in a number of distinctive planning objectives. A naturalized urban environment or urban-rural continuum implied, first of all, a democratization of the country estate and suburb, with their attributes of spaciousness and beauty. Landscape architects sought to bring the country into the city, providing environmental amenities hitherto reserved for those who possessed mobility and wealth. In large measure, this achievement depended upon the development of a comprehensive park-boulevard system which would include not only large rural reservations, but also small neighborhood parks or squares.

Comprehensive park development necessitated long-range, systematic planning. If a city failed to reserve land for future park use according to a definite plan, it would become increasingly difficult to acquire suitable sites at reasonable prices. The ideal of a comprehensive park system directed the attention of landscape architects beyond city limits. They were among the first to emphasize the functional interdependence of city and regional hinterland and to urge the establishment of regional planning agencies. The Boston Metropolitan Park Commission pioneered in American regional planning. As early as the 1890's it voiced the need for cooperative effort among park, water, and sewerage authorities.

In seeking a satisfactory relationship between man, space, and nature in the urban community, landscape architects not only popularized the notion of public planning, but undermined the tyranny of the gridiron subdivision. They stressed, first, the desirability of a differentiated street system. Inspired by the great boulevards of Europe, particularly those of Haussmann's Paris, they advocated their use in American cities to expedite travel, to link the units of the city-regional park system, and to serve as a kind of linear park. Basically, the standardized gridiron plan was incompatible with the urban-rural continuum principle. Often the gridiron was a form of pseudo-planning. It bril-

---

[2] *Report of the Board of Metropolitan Park Commissioners* (Boston, January, 1893), p. 72.

liantly served the purposes of rapid, speculative subdivision and transfer, but sacrificed existing advantages of site and topography. Landscape architects maintained that the principles of picturesque planning were as valid for the ordinary residential subdivision as for the great rural park or country estate.

The romantic suburb became the most extreme, exotic example of the naturalistic residential subdivision. Llewellyn Park (New Jersey), the first, was begun in the ante-bellum period. The romantic suburb was subsequently popularized by Olmsted and Vaux's Riverside (Illinois), where a picturesque informality contrasted sharply with the "constantly repeated right angles, straight lines, and flat surfaces which characterize our large modern town." [3] In its spaciousness, elimination of the corridor street, and integration of human and natural environment, the romantic suburb suggested an entirely new approach to residential design.

The urban-rural continuum principle contributed to one of the great social achievements of the so-called Gilded Age. Between the 1860's and 1890's many American cities established the foundations for their modern park system. New York and Philadelphia had begun in the 1850's with Central Park and Fairmount Park, respectively. Park commissions were later established in Brooklyn, Boston, Detroit, Chicago, Indianapolis, Kansas City, Milwaukee, Minneapolis, St. Paul, and other cities. The significance of these commissions transcended that of the parks they created. They were among the first municipal planning agencies, and marked a major step in the expansion of municipal welfare functions.

In their crusade for parks and open space, landscape architects did not respond solely to esthetic imperatives. They interpreted parks as a means to the creation of an urban environment compatible with health and social stability. Parks and boulevards acted as buffers against the spread of fires. They provided a salubrious relief from the "artificial" stimuli of urban life, and in tenement districts they offered amenities "which the rich win by travel or by living in luxurious country seats." Extensive, embellished open spaces filled a void in the existence of the urban masses, setting in motion the "purest and most ennobling of

[3] "Riverside, Illinois: A Residential Neighborhood Designed over Sixty Years Ago," in *Preliminary Report upon the Proposed Suburban Village at Riverside, Near Chicago, by Olmsted, Vaux and Co.,* ed. Theodora Kimball Hubbard, *Landscape Architecture,* **21** (July, 1931), 274.

external influences." They provided alternatives to "unwholesome, vicious, and destructive methods of seeking recreation." [4] Though they may have exaggerated the social advantages of parks, landscape architects pioneered in efforts to coordinate environmental and social planning in the urban community.

In certain respects, landscape architects and housing reformers pursued similar ends. Both sought to achieve social objectives through environmental melioration. Both favored a greater measure of public decision-making at the expense of private interests. They viewed the tenement park, or playground as an oasis in a concrete jungle, offering sunlight, fresh air, and opportunities to satisfy gregarious instincts in a socially permissible fashion. The park thus served as an instrument of social control.

For housing reformers, however, open space was supplementary to the main objective—enactment of legislation which imposed minimum structural and sanitary standards. In pursuit of restrictive legislation, the housing movement developed close ties with public health officials. Enforcement of housing codes was frequently assigned to health departments. Public health experts were, for obvious reasons, equally concerned with problems of overcrowding, impure water, and faulty sewerage. The accomplishments of housing reformers after 1900 were attributable, in good measure, to their association with the broader public health movement. Confirmation of the germ theory of disease had opened a new era in public health; the claims of housing reformers that substandard housing generated disease were established on a scientific, rather than empirical, basis. The struggle against tuberculosis, rampant in overcrowded, low-income neighborhoods, cemented the alliance between the health and housing movements. Finally, as strongly as any group, health officials endorsed the principle of public environmental control, and in the process greatly enlarged the scope of municipal welfare functions.

Housing and health reformers looked upon restrictive legislation as the key to housing betterment. They also hoped that widespread in-

---

[4] Charles Eliot, *A Report upon the Opportunities for Public Open Spaces in the Metropolitan District of Boston, Massachusetts, Made to the Metropolitan Park Commission, 1892* (Boston, 1893), p. 10; "Report of Egbert L. Viele," *First Annual Report of the Commissioners of Prospect Park, Brooklyn* (January 28, 1861), p. 28; and Frederick L. Olmsted, *The Park for Detroit* (December, 1882), p. 18.

vestment in semi-philanthropic "model" tenements would increase the supply of good, low-cost housing. The Octavia Hill method of housing management represented a third approach. Originating in England, the Octavia Hill method implied resident supervision, high maintenance standards, and some control over the tenants' personal lives. Both the model housing and Octavia Hill schemes were designed, in effect, to withdraw low-income housing from the speculative market. Public service, rather than maximum profit, constituted the rationale for investment. Restrictive legislation, on the other hand, did not substitute for speculative development. It insured, presumably, that housing standards did not drop below statutory minimums. Otherwise, competitive market mechanisms were free to operate.

The Octavia Hill method, of course, did not produce houses. Model tenement schemes never attracted enough investors to seriously challenge the speculative builder. Surplus capital in an expanding economy found more profitable outlets. For all practical purposes, housing remained the province of the petty entrepreneur, tempered by community standards embodied in restrictive legislation. Despite European precedents, few proposals for direct or indirect government subsidy appeared before World War I. Beginning around 1917 a number of architects and housing economists—Edith Elmer Wood, Robert D. Kohn, Frederick L. Ackerman, and Charles H. Whitaker—launched a drive to discredit the "negative" approach to housing in favor of "constructive" European-type legislation. They looked enviously to England, Germany, and Belgium, where public housing, tax exemption, and low-interest loans to cooperatives, limited-dividend companies, or building and loan associations were used to increase the supply of low-cost housing.

Constructive housing legislation in this country was consistently opposed by Lawrence Veiller, the leading apostle of restrictive codes, founder of the National Housing Association, and author of the influential New York State Tenement House Law of 1901. Most city and state housing codes after 1901 were based upon the New York law or the model laws prepared by Veiller and published by the Russell Sage Foundation. Veiller condemned constructive legislation as socialistic and self-defeating in the long run. A limited program of government financial assistance would not supply the need; a massive program would drive out private enterprise entirely and place an enormous burden upon taxpayers.

Under Veiller's leadership the housing movement progressed in organization and effectiveness. Yet restrictive legislation possessed severe limitations. At best it could prevent the worst housing, but could not insure a sufficient supply of good housing at costs or rentals appropriate to the lowest income groups. The same objections raised against government subsidy could apply to restrictive legislation. High standards, rigidly enforced, might discourage private enterprise by cutting profit margins. Restrictive legislation, finally, did not provide adequate guidance for improvements in residential site-planning and design.

In view of the objections to constructive housing legislation in America, the only alternative way to improve housing standards while reducing costs was through progress in construction and design. Few American architects, however, applied their talents to problems of low-cost housing. I. N. Phelps Stokes of New York represented a notable exception. Stokes diverged from the mainstream of American housing reform in stressing design innovation rather than restrictive legislation. The latter, Stokes complained, not only raised costs but also discouraged experimentation and architectural creativity. Stokes linked his proposals for design innovation with an ingenious plan for urban renewal. He proposed to the New York State Tenement House Commission of 1901 that the municipality acquire and raze tenement blocks. The two perimeter strips, about 40 feet wide and running lengthwise along each block, would then be sold to limited-dividend companies, who would build tenements two rooms in depth. The central portion of the blocks would be used for parks and courts.

Nothing came of Stokes' proposals, which implied an expansion of the building unit from the single lot to the block. Working with limited capital and one or a few lots at a time, the builder had no opportunity, let alone desire, to experiment with new designs or groupings of mass and space. Decentralized and technologically primitive, the building industry could not benefit from the economies of scale. It was confronted by a challenge of mass production for which it was unequipped by modern standards of technology and management.

Implicit in the movements discussed was the belief that men could consciously control the physical and social environment of their communities. Competitive market disciplines, the "invisible hand," had not sufficed as a source of order and progress. Landscape architects and conservation leaders sought not only an enlargement of public administrative and welfare functions, but also major reconstructions in community form. The same was true of the City Beautiful movement, which flourished from approximately 1893 to 1910.

The City Beautiful, although important in the evolution of the comprehensive city planning idea in America, has frequently been described as a catastrophe. It allegedly stimulated a neo-classicism which stifled functionalist expression in architecture. An exaggerated emphasis upon municipal ornamentation and embellishment presumably diverted attention from utilitarian concerns in the formative years of American city planning. Despite its limitations, which included a failure to deal with the urban housing problem, the City Beautiful did make several useful contributions to American urban life. It helped incorporate the park movement of the nineteenth century into twentieth-century city planning. Landscape architects such as Charles M. Robinson and George E. Kessler were conspicuous among the leaders of the City Beautiful. Few of their plans lacked provision for extensive park-boulevard development. Through their work, in part, the urban-rural continuum principle entered the mainstream of twentieth-century planning. The almost universal interest in park improvement suggests, furthermore, that the City Beautiful was not entirely devoid of utilitarian or social significance. Similarly, though City Beautiful contributions to housing betterment were minimal, the movement encouraged municipal regulation of eyesores or nuisances: bill-board displays, poles, noise, and overhead wires. In the Brunner-Carrère plan for Grand Rapids, Michigan (1909), one even finds early proposals for comprehensive zoning.

Probably the most distinctive legacy of the City Beautiful was the ideal it embodied of the city as a deliberate work of art. It aspired to universalize the beauty and planned unity which Americans had perceived in the Chicago World's Fair of 1893. The dream city which had risen along Chicago's lake front struck with the force of revelation: "The fair! The fair! Never had the name such significance before. Fairest of all the world's present sights it is. A city of palaces set in spaces of emerald, reflected in shining lengths of water which stretch in undulating lines under flat arches of marble bridges, and along banks planted with consummate skill." The Fair's vital lesson was the supreme "need of design and plan for whole cities," now that "everyone saw plainly that, though a pond be beautiful, a grassy lawn or bank beautiful, a building beautiful, all of these elements wrought into a harmonious design attain another and greater beauty, and that the beauty of the whole is superior to that of each of the several parts of the composition exploited separately." [5] The ephemeral White City stimulated a mood of dissatisfaction with the "awful monotony of ugliness" which reigned in the real cities where people lived and worked. This mood the City Beautiful translated into a quest for communities planned as works of art.

The ideal of the city as a work of art invigorated the tradition of civic design which extended back to colonial Williamsburg, Annapolis, and, not least, L'Enfant's Washington. It was necessary, however, to divest this tradition of its aristocratic connotations. Prophets of the City Beautiful thus assured Americans that the proposed civic centers, grand boulevards, and sculptural and artistic embellishments were truly democratic in contrast to the "work of art in its secluded gallery." [6] Such amenities expressed the pride of a democratic people in their communities and, like public parks, insured equal access to advantages once reserved for the affluent. The City Beautiful elevated public standards of taste and inspired a civic loyalty which transcended ethnic and class fragmentation.

The City Beautiful led to the preparation of plans for numerous American communities. These schemes usually ignored housing and other social problems, but the City Beautiful nonetheless performed a valuable service in introducing new environmental ideals. It popularized the notion that the city was more than an economic machine and that planning was necessary to prevent further visual deterioration. The City Beautiful aspired, through planning, to reconcile industrialization with the great Renaissance-Baroque and indigenous traditions of urban beautification.

A challenge to contemporary urban form, more profound in its social implications than the City Beautiful, came from the Garden City movement. First proposed by Ebenezer Howard of England in 1898, the Garden City was conceived as an alternative to the Victorian industrial city. The scheme appealed to planners disillusioned with the

[5] Candace Wheeler, "A Dream City," *Harper's Magazine,* **86** (May, 1893), 833; and Daniel H. Burnham, "White City and Capital City," *Century Magazine,* **63** (February, 1902), 619.

[6] Frederick S. Lamb, "Municipal Art," *Municipal Affairs,* **1** (December, 1897), 682.

visual and social fruits of speculative capitalism in the urban setting; and to others who had lost confidence in market disciplines as a source of urban order. It interested land and tax reformers who viewed slum housing as an inevitable consequence of high land values fostered by speculation and overcrowding. The opportunities for large-scale planning attracted socially oriented architects who believed that the maximum effectiveness of their profession depended upon the design of total environments rather than fragments.

Howard and his collaborators attempted to demonstrate at Letchworth, England the viability of Garden City principles: (1) urban decentralization; (2) the establishment of cities limited in size, but possessing a balanced agricultural-industrial economy; (3) use of a surrounding greenbelt to help limit size, and to serve as an agricultural-recreational area; (4) cooperative landholding to insure that the community rather than private individuals benefited from appreciation of land values; and (5) the economic and social advantages of large-scale planning. In the questions it raised about the form and structure of cities, and in the solutions proposed, the Garden City was perhaps the most radical of the twentieth-century urban reform movements. Letchworth, followed by Welwyn Garden City (and the New Towns after World War II), demonstrated that the Garden City represented a practical radicalism.

The Garden City, a formidable undertaking, made little progress in the United States. Americans tended to emphasize the more limited "garden suburb" as better suited to immediate, widespread application. They frequently cited England's Bournville and Port Sunlight as examples of the planned industrial garden suburb. Hampstead Garden Suburb served as a demonstration of good residential design. In their zeal to promote low-density model communities which would relieve population pressures in older cities, Americans performed something of a disservice to the Garden City. They tended to identify it with almost any variety of low-density suburban subdivision whether or not it satisfied Howard's criteria. The Garden City idea in the early American planning movement served primarily as a stimulus for more limited schemes of residential or industrial decentralization.

In seeking to convince businessmen, philanthropists, and commercial developers of the desirability of model garden communities, American reformers cited German as well as English experience. They pointed to the Krupp towns of Alfredshof and Altenhof, near Essen, and Hellerau, outside Dresden, as examples of planned worker colonies. These German and English garden communities demonstrated to their satisfaction that a practical alternative to further metropolitan centralization existed. The advantages of garden suburb-development included efficient land-use, low density, provision for recreational needs, and prevalence of the private home rather than the multi-family tenement.

American precedents for model community planning, residential or otherwise, were sparse. The romantic suburb such as Riverside, Illinois, had only limited applicability. More practical as models were the few "essentially commercial developments, usually of high-grade property, as exemplified at Garden City, L.I., and Roland Park, in the suburbs of Baltimore." A few additional semi-philanthropic and commercial subdivisions of a model variety appeared after 1910. Sponsored by the Russell Sage Foundation as a residential suburb for persons of "modest means," Forest Hills Gardens (Long Island) was meant to demonstrate the application of "scientific, aesthetic, and economic principles and methods to the problem of housing civilization." [7] Even though attractive commercial subdivisions such as Forest Hills Gardens, the J. C. Nichols Country Club District (Kansas City), and Shaker Heights (Cleveland) were pale reflections of the Garden City, they served a useful purpose. They displayed the advantages of large-scale development in which streets and lots were related to "topography, building site, strategic lines of communication, uses or needs." [8]

Much interest in planned garden communities in the early twentieth century focused upon model industrial towns. Presumably, businessmen possessed not only the necessary capital, but also concrete incentives such as lower rents, more space, and significantly, a stable labor force. Nonetheless, the outstanding example of a planned industrial community in the nineteenth century may have served ultimately to discourage business firms from assuming responsibility for town development. Despite its superior physical environment, Pullman, Illinois, had not averted labor strife in the 1890's. If anything, workers resented the Pullman Company's benevolent feudalism. Employers could cite the Pullman experience in answer to the reformer's argument

[7] Grosvenor Atterbury, "Model Towns in America," *Scribner's Magazine,* 52 (July, 1912), 21, 25.
[8] J. C. Nichols, "Financial Effect of Good Planning in Land Subdivision," National Conference on City Planning, *Proceedings* (1916), p. 97.

that housing was a legitimate concern of industry. Community planning always remained incidental to production. It was seen as a necessary evil rather than an opportunity to discharge social obligations or to pioneer in residential design.

A few companies did hire prominent architects to design new industrial towns. John Nolen was particularly prominent in this work. He prepared the plan for the garden village of the Mount Union Refractories Company at Kistler, Pennsylvania, and was also the planner for Kingsport, Tennessee. The outstanding opportunity for advanced industrial town planning was lost, however, in the founding of Gary, Indiana, by the United States Steel Corporation. By the 1920's there were only a few garden spots in the dreary desert of American industrial towns, and a handful of experiments in residential subdivision (which rarely benefited low-income groups). This limited achievement demonstrated the inadequacies of a reform program dependent upon the vision or altruism of philanthropists, employers, and commercial developers.

The concept of planned urban growth was firmly established in America by the close of the first decade of the twentieth century. In the context of the broader social reform crusade of the Progressive era, the various movements discussed helped undermine faith in competitive market disciplines as the primary source of urban progress. Professional city planning, an institutional expression of the desire for conscious, rational control of the urban environment, emerged after 1909. That year witnessed the founding of the National Conference on City Planning, followed by the American City Planning Institute in 1917. A number of universities included planning courses in their curricula. Many cities created planning commissions, usually in the form of an independent citizens body.

Following New York City's comprehensive zoning resolution of 1916, hundreds of communities enacted similar legislation. It became the planner's key technical tool, necessary for control of urban land use, but one whose limitations were not clearly recognized in the early years. Zoning statutes could be manipulated for purposes of racial or class segregation. Equally important, zoning was negative in character, like restrictive housing legislation. It could prevent the worst consequences of indiscriminate land-use, perhaps, but it could not insure good site-

planning and residential design. Like housing codes based upon speci-
fication rather than performance standards, zoning could thwart creativity and experimentation.

The era of professional planning, particularly by the 1920's, was
marked by a gradual transformation of the planners' role from reformer
to technician. Prior to World War I, the planner was necessarily a
social reformer: he sought to impose land-use and other public controls
over the urban environment, where none had existed previously. He
had to justify planning as a necessary administrative function in the
modern urban community. In the early years professional planning
was affiliated with the parks, City Beautiful, Garden City, housing and
other municipal reform movements which espoused normative goals
and broadened the planner's perception of his function. Increasingly,
however, the professional planner evolved into a technician who mini-
mized normative goals—structural or institutional innovation—and became the prophet of the "City Scientific" or "City Efficient." Technical
matters relating to zoning, law, finance, capital expenditure, and transportation became his province. He did not seek fundamental changes
in urban form and structure, but projected existing demographic and
institutional trends into the future as a basis for planning.

The emergence of planning as a profession coincided with a
municipal efficiency crusade. Bureaus of Municipal Research were
established in numerous cities in the early twentieth century. Commission and city manager plans of government were instituted with
the somewhat contradictory goals of regenerating municipal democracy
and enlarging the role of the expert. These developments evolved from
and nurtured the belief that the "proper administration of cities is as
much of a scientific procedure as is that of directing the affairs of a
large business institution, for a city is just as much of a unit as is a
business concern." [9] The planner evolved as a kind of municipal efficiency expert, in charge of the physical plant.

The planner's identification with the municipal efficiency movement, the "City Scientific," helps explain his conservative viewpoint.
Professionalization served as another constraint. Prior to the 1920's,
planning consisted of a loose agglomeration of architects, engineers,
and civic reformers who varied in background and preparation. For all
practical purposes, the planner defined his own function. With the

[9] The City Plan Commission, *City Planning for Newark* (Newark, N.J.,
1913), p. 3.

development of professional training and association came efforts to define skills, create a group identity, channel career opportunities, and determine the appropriate administrative setting for planning in the municipal hierarchy. Such rationalization, in turn, served to discourage broad reform objectives in favor of more limited goals appropriate to professional technical skills and career opportunities.

Significant in explaining the planner's role transformation by the 1920's was his increasing preoccupation with transportation problems. Planning emerged as a profession at the same time that the automobile came into widespread use. Improvements in street and circulation patterns took high priority. The transportation challenge enabled planners to exercise their technical skills and demonstrate their usefulness without challenging the institutional status quo. The problem of moving the urban population absorbed the planner's attention, resulting in an epidemic of proposals for street widening, traffic control, and rerouting of vehicles. Narrow streets of the pre-automobile age had become obsolete; relief from traffic congestion was the "need in cities which is attracting the most attention." [10]

As the planning profession's concern for housing and related social issues diminished towards the 1920's, the housing movement itself floundered. World War I sharply inflated housing costs, producing severe shortages throughout the nation. The speculative developer withdrew from the low-income market. In a period of scarcity and rising costs, restrictive legislation became not only ineffectual, but also irrelevant. It was not surprising that the vigorous housing reform movement of the Progressive era declined. It had reached a cul-de-sac. Restrictive legislation could not build houses, but Americans were not yet prepared to concede the necessity for government financial participation. The demonstrable inadequacies of restrictive legislation in the early 1920's did, however, lead to serious consideration of proposals for "constructive" legislation and a couple of significant experiments.

Proposals for government involvement in housing finance were scarce prior to World War I. President Roosevelt's Homes Commission, appointed in 1908, attempted to deal with the District of Columbia's notorious alley slums. But it could not acquire Congressional approval for the low-interest loans to limited-dividend companies which it rec-

[10] John Nolen, *Lancaster, Pennsylvania, Comprehensive City Plan* (Lancaster, Pa.: City Planning Commission of Lancaster, 1929), p. 30.

ommended. Neither did Congress approve bills introduced into the House in 1913 and 1915 authorizing the use of postal savings deposits for housing loans. One minor achievement was a 1915 Oklahoma law authorizing home loans of up to $2000 by the Commissioners of the Land Office.

The most significant pre-war experiment in constructive legislation took place in Massachusetts, where a Homestead Commission had been established in 1911. Influenced by the state-assisted "back-to-the-land" movement in Australia and New Zealand, the Commission urged that Massachusetts finance a suburban demonstration project. It hoped to prove that good homes and garden plots could be erected for workers at a "reasonable profit." A successful demonstration would assist in achieving the Commission's chief goal—reversal of the trend toward urban concentration, with its many environmental and social evils. The Commission succeeded in winning a $50,000 appropriation which it used to build twelve homes in Lowell. Abolished shortly thereafter, the Massachusetts Homestead Commission transcended in significance the few homes it produced. It not only pioneered in constructive housing legislation, but also invariably related housing to broader regional considerations such as the urban-rural balance of population. The Commission stressed the economic and social advantages of careful site-planning, and in 1913 it sponsored a mandatory planning law for Massachusetts cities.

Begun after the United States entered World War I, the Commission's Lowell project was quickly overshadowed by the federal housing program of 1918-19. A serious housing shortage, particularly in armaments and ship-building centers, had forced the federal government to act in the interests of war production efficiency. Operating through the U.S. Housing Corporation and the Emergency Fleet Corporation of the U.S. Shipping Board, the government built homes for several thousand families. Despite the pressures of war-time haste, and shortages of labor and materials, the federal program marked a turning point in American housing. For the first time it enabled architects such as Robert D. Kohn, Frederick L. Ackerman, and Henry Wright to experiment extensively with the large-scale community planning identified with the Garden City and suburbs of England. It established a precedent for federal aid to housing, and demonstrated that government financial assistance combined with large-scale residential planning might radically improve housing conditions in American cities.

The acute housing shortage which followed the war reached its peak between 1919 and 1921, stimulating numerous proposals for government assistance. Only California, however, responded in a direct, constructive manner. The Veterans' Farm and Home Purchase Act of 1921 authorized state purchase or construction of homes and farms for sale to veterans on liberal credit terms. California invested $24 million in nearly 5,000 homes and 250 farms within seven years. Ambitious by the standards of the time, the program lacked the communitarian features of California's earlier venture in constructive housing legislation. A Land Settlement Act of 1917, based upon the recommendations of a Commission on Land Colonization and Rural Credits, had established a Land Settlement Board which sponsored the two farm villages of Durham and Delhi.

In New York State the immediate response to the post-war housing crisis consisted of a series of rent control measures and a tax exemption law which failed to limit profits or rentals. It proved to be a speculative bonanza which increased the housing supply in New York City but did not benefit low-income groups. A continued shortage of low-cost housing, particularly in the Metropolis, and the efforts of the New York State Commission of Housing and Regional Planning, led finally to the Limited-Dividend Housing Act of 1926. This measure authorized tax exemptions for companies approved by a State Board of Housing. The legislature, unfortunately, had eliminated provision for a state housing bank to supply low-cost capital. Tax exemption alone produced only a handful of apartment projects, all in New York City. The New York State Housing Law of 1926 was nonetheless significant. It combined government financial assistance with efforts through the State Board of Housing to encourage good site-planning of multi-family dwellings.

The Regional Planning Association of America (RPAA), organized in 1923, had been closely identified with the struggle to launch a constructive housing program in New York State. Throughout its ten-year existence, the RPAA remained a small, informal group, the inner circle of which consisted of three architects (Clarence S. Stein, Henry Wright, and Frederick L. Ackerman), Benton MacKaye, a forester and conservationist, and Lewis Mumford. The RPAA marked both the end and beginning of an era in housing and planning. Its program was rooted, in part, in the reform movements of the late nineteenth century and Progressive period: conservation, landscape architecture and park planning, the Garden City, housing betterment. An ideological continuity existed in the RPAA's revolt against speculative capitalism. It voiced, in an extreme way, earlier aspirations to substitute the disciplines of the expert—architectural, planning, and welfare—for those of the market.

Out of these earlier traditions, blended with a number of European influences, the RPAA forged a unique, creative synthesis. Best described as "community planning," this synthesis consisted of a unified approach to three variables which profoundly influenced the form and growth of cities: residential site-planning practices, housing costs, and the regional distribution of population, resources, and institutions. In the area of residential planning, the RPAA stressed the economic and social advantages of large-scale or "quanta" development. The group aspired, second, to combine new residential planning techniques with painstaking cost analysis. It became clear, in this connection, that the supply and cost of capital was critical; consequently, the RPAA became identified with efforts to acquire through government an ample supply of low-cost capital for home-building. Finally, the RPAA urged a regional reconstruction which encompassed the establishment of Garden Cities or New Towns, the renewal of existing cities (made economically feasible through decentralization), and preservation of the countryside.

In the case of large-scale or quanta development, the primary influence was the Garden City. It suggested to members of the RPAA the desirability of a new orientation to urban growth. They went beyond Howard's critique of metropolitan agglomeration, however, to propose not only New Towns but also a generalized process of cellular, organic city-building—by "superblock" and neighborhood units as well as entire communities. The work of Raymond Unwin and Barry Parker at Letchworth Garden City, the suburbs of Hampstead and Earswick, and the British war-housing communities provided them with concrete demonstrations in quanta planning. It was only through enlargement of the development unit, the RPAA maintained, that the architect or planner could exploit existing advantages of site and topography; benefit from the economies of scale, including street and utility expenditures; efficiently group open space; and provide in advance for the necessary complement of social and recreational facilities.

Community planning precedents in America which influenced the

RPAA included the federal housing program of World War I and superior examples of industrial town development: Kingsport, Tennessee; Kistler, Pennsylvania; Neponset Garden Village, East Walpole, Massachusetts; Tyrone, New Mexico; and Indian Hill Village, Worcester, Massachusetts. Of great importance was the tradition of the romantic and garden suburb. Here the corridor street was eliminated, the subdivision scale enlarged, and the human residence integrated into its naturalistic setting. The superblock design, used by Wright and Stein at Radburn (New Jersey) and Chatham Village (Pittsburgh), incorporated all these principles. In these communities, the architects combined the quanta planning tradition and the urban-rural continuum ideal as a basis for residential subdivision.

The RPAA insisted that unified, large-scale development produced a residential environment biologically and visually superior to that of the small speculative builder, whose narrow-lot flats spanned monotonous gridiron streets. Equally important, in the eyes of the RPAA, the cellular principle of planned urban growth was better suited to the ordinary family needs of the modern urban population. If the population of residential units was known in advance, and development was unified, it was easier to plan for necessary social and commercial facilities. A distinct advantage in the use of the superblock, differentiated street system and cul-de-sac (as at Radburn and Chatham Village) was the separation of pedestrian and vehicular traffic. The efficient grouping of open space in the form of extensive recreational facilities and the superblock interior park represented another advantage of quanta planning. Members of the RPAA believed that these amenities, incorporated into the texture of the residential design, were a necessary response to the changing ratio between work and leisure time in the twentieth century. Finally, the RPAA hoped that urban growth along cellular lines would stimulate civic association. Spatially defined, visually attractive residential environments might counteract, to some extent, the centrifugal pressures of modern urban life. Such environments might reduce the vast abstraction of the city to the more comprehensible scale of the block and neighborhood. These efforts to coordinate physical and social planning were central to the RPAA's synthesis. In this respect, it diverged from the mainstream of professional planning.

Always concerned with practical matters of cost, members of the RPAA came to view the scarcity of low-interest capital as a major obstacle to housing betterment. Indeed, urban development by quanta units required great concentrations of capital in contrast to that needed by the small, speculative builder, who worked on a shoe-string equity. As mentioned earlier, the RPAA worked to establish permanent programs of government financial assistance. If limited-dividend or cooperative housing companies could be supplied with sufficient capital, the low- and even middle-income housing market might be withdrawn from the speculative sphere altogether. In essence, the RPAA aspired to transform urban land and housing into public utilities rather than commodities fluctuating in a competitive market system.

The RPAA's community planning synthesis hinged, ultimately, upon its ideals of regional reconstruction. Identified particularly with Lewis Mumford and Benton MacKaye, the regional program drew from a variety of European and American sources. Mumford was greatly influenced by the Scottish biologist and planner, Patrick Geddes, who emphasized the interdependence of city and country and aspired to a regional unity of "place, work, and folk—environment, function, and organism." [11] Mumford was influenced also by the French regionalist tradition, extending from the Provençal romantics of the mid-nineteenth century through efforts to establish the region as an administrative, economic and cultural unit in the early twentieth century. French regional geographers such as Vidal de la Blanche directed Mumford's attention to the ecology of regions and the manner in which human institutions affected the balance of nature. In this country the colonial New England farm-village provided him with clues to regional development. The early New Englanders had adopted a pattern of nucleated settlement. Communities, loosely federated in a regional Congregational polity, were limited in size, but were economically balanced and inclusive in terms of necessary religious-civic institutions. From America Mumford also drew liberally upon the work of George Perkins Marsh, the nineteenth-century geographer who protested against the wanton exploitation of America's natural resources and warned of the consequences resulting from thoughtless disruption of nature's equilibrium.

A forester by profession, a New Englander by adoption, Benton MacKaye personified the indigenous regional tradition. His regional theory, expressed in the *New Exploration* (1928), combined the com-

---

[11] Patrick Geddes, *Cities in Evolution: An Introduction to the Town Planning Movement and to the Study of Civics* (London, 1915), p. 198.

munitarian values of the New England farm-village, the romantic naturalism of Thoreau, and the conservationist emphasis upon scientific resource development. MacKaye was the originator of the famed Appalachian Trail and an advocate of rural electrification.

The RPAA claimed that the gasoline engine and electric power provided a technological basis for regional reconstruction. The question, essentially, was whether the residential and industrialization decentralization already in progress would be controlled, or whether it would result in a formless, low-density suburban diffusion which devoured land and produced community fragments lacking a sound economic base. The RPAA believed that this kind of decentralization was no suitable alternative to the metropolitan centralization of the nineteenth century. "Dinosaur" cities, as Stein described great agglomerations such as New York and Chicago, were neither necessary nor efficient in light of modern technology. In order to survive, they required vast overheads in the form of expenditures for transit and utility systems. Congestion of population forced intensive land utilization, creating additional overheads through inflated property values. This led to further congestion, and more intensive land use, in an endless cycle. The process of speculative appreciation made it difficult to produce low-cost, low-density housing and discouraged liberal acquisition of land for recreational or civic purposes.

As an alternative to metropolitan centralization and suburban diffusion, the RPAA proposed the "regional city." By regional city the RPAA meant not some ideal form, but rather a new orientation to city-building in the regional context. The term suggested a regional grouping of community types of all kinds, large and small, based upon a planned regional balance of population, resources, and institutions. In the regional city pattern, size would be a function of explicit social objectives.

The RPAA marked the beginning and end of an era. It climaxed the efforts, launched in the late nineteenth century, to establish public controls over urban form and land-use. This implied a greater decision-making role for government agencies and social technicians at the expense of private business interests. In effect, the RPAA embodied the ideal of administered, planned urban growth which emerged during the Progressive period. On the other hand, the community planning synthesis of the RPAA represented a wholly new approach to urban form and social organization. Progressive era reformers aspired to ameliorate the environmental and social pathologies of existing cities; the RPAA maintained that this could not be accomplished without fundamental innovations in residential design and housing finance in a context of regional planning.

ROY LUBOVE

part one

CONSERVATION
AND
COMMUNITY

Conservation is often equated with the limited goal of resource and wildlife protection. Actually, the historical significance of the conservation movement centers on its effort to establish the principle of scientific resource utilization. This principle, applicable to an urban as well as to a rural setting, had important implications for city and regional planning. Urban land is among the most valuable of resources; decisions affecting land-use profoundly influence the life of a city.

The two documents in this section illustrate that conservation leaders consciously attempted to relate resource policy and social organization. Benton MacKaye began his report on employment and resources while a member of the U.S. Forest Service. This little-known work represents one of the most imaginative expressions of conservationist ideals. The selections that follow, dealing specifically with agricultural and timber policy, demonstrate clearly that the conservationist was also a community-builder, a pioneer in efforts to coordinate physical and social planning.

The *Report* of the California Commission led to a novel experiment in community-building. The Commission chairman, Elwood Mead, was an engineer and irrigation authority, long associated with the conservation movement. Complaining of the decay of rural community life, the Commission recommended a systematic state land settlement or colonization policy. A Land Settlement Act in 1917 authorized the appointment of a Land Settlement Board which sponsored two farm communities (Durham Land Settlement in Butte County north of Sacramento, and Delhi Settlement, in the San Joaquin Valley south of Sacramento).

The community planning policies represented by MacKaye and the California Commission contrasted sharply with the homestead tradition of dispersed agricultural settlement.

Land Colonization and Rural Credits

State of California

CONCLUSIONS AND RECOMMENDATIONS

Need for State Land Settlement Policy

The colonization and development of the unpeopled farm lands of California is of such importance to all the people of the state that it should not be left to the separate action of landowners, but should be shaped in part by the carefully thought out purposeful action of all the people. This means that the state should have a land settlement policy and deal with this matter as a public problem.

Other Countries Have a Lesson for Us

The progress being made by other nations in improving agricultural methods, in uplifting agricultural workers, and in affording all who are fitted for it by industry and character, the opportunity to enjoy landed independence has a lesson for this country which ought not be ignored. Such progress is making other countries better places to live in, increasing their industrial efficiency and their political and social strength, and making them dangerous commercial competitors. We do not believe that this country will be content to let older nations surpass us in those

Report of the Commission on Land Colonization and Rural Credits of the State of California, November 29, 1916 (Sacramento, 1916), pp. 82-87. The sources, as reproduced here, differ little from the originals. Footnotes and graphic material have been deleted, occasional spelling errors corrected, and minor changes made in punctuation.

things which contribute to the welfare of the rural masses. Our immense unpeopled estates give us an opportunity to surpass all European countries except Russia in the extent of rural development. Each of these estates is a blank leaf on which we may write whatever record we choose.

Selfish Individualism or Community Good?

We may perpetuate a selfish and short-sighted individualism. We may try to make all we can out of the gifts of nature. We may charge everyone who comes here all that can be collected for the sunshine, scenery, society, and soil. We may, by extending alien tenantry and ignoring the social needs of farm labor, create slums in the country while we collect high rents.

Or by regarding colonization and the creation of rural communities as a trust, we may create agricultural colonies filled with people who will make this a state where the best people in this country will want to live. We may only do this, however, if the diversion of our rivers, the selection of land for colonies, and the methods of development are planned and directed by the best thought and intelligence of the time. We shall achieve nothing by leaving these things to blind chance.

In this report attention has been called to undesirable conditions only when it was necessary to show the manner and degree in which private unregulated colonization has failed and the need for displacing it by something wiser and better.

STATE SUPERVISION OF SETTLEMENT

It is believed that every interest which needs consideration would be benefited by providing for state supervision of colonization. There is some difficulty in accomplishing this because it ought not to embrace ordinary sales of land from one person to another, but only include those enterprises which assume sufficient magnitude to have public importance and in which settlers who are unacquainted with local conditions are sought from the outside or from a particular neighborhood. Such supervision should aim to accomplish the following results:

1. To provide that adequate attention has been given to water supplies and drainage in irrigated areas
2. That the land is suited to the purposes for which it is being sold
3. That there is no misrepresentation in the advertising

Aim and Result of State Supervision

It should also aim to aid those engaged in colonization by pointing out features in the plan they are following which are likely to lead to failure. Such state supervision would in no way hamper development, but by preventing misrepresentation and giving new colonization enterprises the benefit of a wider experience would protect them from mistakes and also safeguard the settler.

It would promote development by strengthening confidence in our advertising statements abroad, but it will not of itself lead to the adoption of the best features of the land settlement systems of other countries. Private companies will not give the terms of Denmark, Germany, or Australia until it has been demonstrated here that such terms can be given with safety. They will not provide homes for farm laborers until shown that these homes will be paid for and be a community asset. No country has adopted modern settlement methods until its government took the initiative and showed the value of them. We can not expect California to be an exception.

More Generous Personal Credit System Necessary

In the past settlers and land settlement have been helped by the large increase in land prices which accompanied development. This made it possible to borrow money for improvements or to sell a part of the original purchase for nearly the first cost of the whole area. This aid can not be relied upon in the future and we must replace it by a more generous personal credit system and by introducing more efficient and cheaper methods of preparing farms for intensive cultivation.

The experience of other countries and of some colonization enterprises in this country indicates that it is cheaper for an organization having ample capital to level and seed the land and finance the building of houses than to leave the work to the individual settler.

Longer Terms for Payment Necessary

The experience of other countries is to the effect that a longer time in which to pay for farms than has been given in California is desirable. The tendency in Canada is to make the payment period not less than 20 years. In European countries it varies from 30 to 75 years.

The following suggestions are made as to the future financing of settlers in California:

1. Give 20 to 30 years' time in which to pay for land.
2. After the initial payment require no further payment on principal for the first two years, but stipulate in the selling contract the character of the improvements which must be made.
3. Have the payments of land amortized and the amount of the annual or semiannual payments equal throughout the entire period.

State Bureaus of Information

It also seems desirable that the state should aid colonization by establishing one or more offices in the state where information regarding land in approved colony enterprises could be obtained.

The state might also, as West Virginia is now doing, distribute printed lists of land in enterprises that are approved, giving the conditions of settlement and the kind of crops which might be grown.

COLONIZATION BY THE STATE

It is believed that over a considerable part of this country the different states will soon have joined other enlightened countries in making colonization a public matter. In the East it will be done to lessen tenant farming and improve agricultural practices; in the West as the best method of rapidly settling unoccupied and uncultivated land.

The Tendency toward State Settlement in This Country

The tendency towards the adoption of this policy in the West is shown by the decision of the United States Reclamation Service to level and improve farms before offering them for settlement; in the introductions and hearings on the Crosser Bill, which, if enacted, will go farther than even Denmark and Germany in financing settlers on public lands; and in the report of the Cooperative Land Settlement Board in Wyoming, which has recommended that the federal government build irrigation works and that the state subdivide the land, select the settlers and finance them in making their necessary improvements. It is understood that this report has the support of the state authorities in Wyoming and that legislation to carry it into effect is being framed.

Possibility of State Influence in California

The immense area of land in the large estates of California would make progress too slow if it depended entirely on action by the state, but the state can do more than any other single influence to promote the adoption of right policies by making a demonstration in colonization for the purpose of showing how superior carefully thought out development is to that where only local or immediate benefits are considered.

The Need for an Educational Demonstration by the State

The state which blazes the trail in scientific colonization will secure a prominence and establish a moral leadership that will be of great value in attracting desirable settlers. No state has more to gain from such leadership than has California. A concrete working example in this state of the methods and policies which have transformed rural life and immensely improved agricultural practices in Denmark, Ireland, Germany, Australia, and New Zealand would do more than any other single influence to insure future agricultural progress along right lines. In no other way can the owners of large estates be so effectively shown what to do and what to avoid. In no other way can the present tendency to create here a great alien land tenantry be more certainly checked. If the state were to purchase, subdivide, and settle 10,000 acres, its action would be watched by the whole world. It is entirely feasible to make this educational demonstration commercially profitable. It can be made to pay its way, so as to cost the taxpayer nothing. Such result has been achieved in the countries whose state systems have been held up as examples; there is no reason to doubt our ability to be equally efficient and successful.

DEMONSTRATION SHOULD BE ON A COMMERCIAL SCALE

An area of about 10,000 acres is suggested, because this area can be more economically and effectively managed than a smaller one; and its results would be of more general value. A larger area is not advised because of the cost.

Out of such an area there would have to be deducted, let us say, 300 acres for roads, canals, schoolhouses, and recreation grounds; 100 acres for farm laborers' allotments and a few small orchards and gardens. This would leave 9,600 acres, or enough for about two hundred farms varying in size from 20 to 100 acres.

If these two hundred farms were all settled by alert, ambitious young men and women, there would be a community that would be to agriculture in California what the Greeley Colony was to irrigated farming in Colorado. The value of this demonstration would be increased by restricting settlement to qualified applicants between the ages of eighteen and thirty, men of experience and training, no one to be eligible who owns farm land elsewhere in the state, nor who has not had at least one year's farming experience, and who can not within six months become an actual resident and cultivator of his farm.

In planning colonies the state should follow the main working features of the plans which have succeeded best elsewhere. We believe that if the plans included the following the results would be entirely satisfactory:

The land to be sold on 36 years' time, with an initial cash payment of 5 per cent, with interest payments of 4½ per cent and amortized annual payments of principal of 1½ per cent beginning at the end of the fourth year, the settler to pay for his land and have a clear title in the payment period by paying 4½ per cent on the cost the first four years and 6 per cent on the cost the remaining 32 years. Each settler should be required to have capital enough to pay, in cash, one-fourth the cost of all improvements made by the state; payment of the remainder of the cost of improvements to be amortized and bear the same interest as the payments on land. With these terms of payment for land and improvements it is believed that existing financial institutions can give whatever credit is necessary in buying equipment, including dairy cows.

The Features of a State Colony

The selection of colonists should be entrusted to a board, the subsequent business management to be in the hands of a single competent superintendent reporting to this board. The State Agricultural College should make systematic provision for giving advice and information regarding farm management and cultivation. The superintendent would give advice about buying livestock and equipping farms. The state should, by contract, build houses, level land for irrigation or loan money to settlers on insurable improvements carried out under the direction and to the satisfaction of the authorities in control, a conservative maximum limit to be fixed.

The prices of farms after subdivision should be so adjusted as to pay for land lost in roads and canals, also interest on the cost of the land between time of subdivision and time of settlement and all other incidental expenses. In Australia 15 per cent was sufficient to cover the above items.

The selection of the land should be entrusted to an expert committee, the purpose being not to enhance or depress prices, but to buy land at its productive value. If this were understood, it would be a guarantee to settlers that they were getting their money's worth. The character of various state commissions shows that there will be no difficulty in the appointment of one in whom the public would have implicit confidence, and who would see that a price was paid for land which would be fair to landowners and settlers alike. The land might be paid for with state bonds bearing, say 4 per cent interest, or bought under a contract by which the landowner would give deeds direct to the settler, the state guaranteeing his payments and having the right to complete the purchase and enter into full ownership at any time deemed advisable. Existing state authorities could plan the works for a water supply, subdivide the area and fix the size of farms. In financing the settlers the amount of capital to be provided can be greatly reduced by making full use of the loaning possibilities of the Federal Farm Loan Act.

State Settlement in Accord with Tendency of Our Time

These departures from the methods and policies under which the state has reached its present wealth and greatness are in accordance with the changing tendencies of our time. Before the beginning of the present war and more rapidly since its beginning the leading nations of the world are organizing all their resources and their industries, so as to eliminate waste, promote efficiency and give the broadest possible diffusion of opportunities. Making settlement a public matter and using the wisdom and experience of the world in shaping our methods and policies will not only attract people here, but will do more to make California a desirable place to live in and secure a better use of our resources than can be accomplished in any other way.

Respectfully submitted,

(Signed) ELWOOD MEAD, *Chairman*
HARRIS WEINSTOCK
DAVID P. BARROWS
MORTIMER FLEISHHACKER
CHESTER ROWELL

DAVID N. MORGAN, *Secretary*

Employment and Natural Resources

Benton MacKaye

DEVELOPMENT OF AGRICULTURAL LANDS

One-fourth of the area of the United States (478 million acres) is improved agricultural land; another fourth of the country (475 million acres) is, according to estimates, capable of being improved for farming purposes. More than one-fourth of the country's area (510 million acres) consists of grazing land; the remainder consists for the most part of permanent forest land. Of the 475 million acres still to be developed for farming purposes, over 80 per cent occurs within present farm boundaries—chiefly in the settled portions of the Central States and elsewhere in the eastern half of the country. The remainder (85 million acres) consists of reclaimable waste lands outside of present farm bounds. Only a small portion of profitable farm land remains on the public domain.

Agricultural land on the western public domain formed, perhaps, the main opportunity for alternative employment and a new career to the average worker 50 years ago. This land was taken up for the most part through the homestead law of 1862. Under the terms of this law the settler could get from the Government, in fee simple and without charge, a total of 160 acres of land on condition of maintaining a residence thereon for a term of years and making certain improvements.

Benton MacKaye, *Employment and Natural Resources: Possibilities of Making New Opportunities for Employment through the Settlement and Development of Agricultural and Forest Lands and Other Resources,* United States Department of Labor, Office of the Secretary (Washington, D.C.: Government Printing Office, 1919), pp. 17, 18, 21-23.

Need of Colonization

One grave objection to the homestead law was (and is) the principle upon which it was based, namely, that raw land without improvements is all the settler needs wherewith to make for himself a farm and a home. In the fertile portions of the open prairie requiring little or no reclamation, and in favorable spots elsewhere, the settler who was hardened to the pioneer life was, to be sure, often able to equip himself for farming through his single-handed methods. But he was always under the heavy handicap that comes from the lack of cooperative effort, and his less fortunate or less robust comrade was unable to keep up. Nor did the aid through irrigation provided for in the reclamation act of 1902, or the general processes of reclamation as practiced—whether on the arid, swamp, or cut-over lands—do as much as was generally expected to improve the pioneer's condition. This was because the processes were not carried far enough. It is not enough merely to provide desert land with needed water or to drain swamp land of surplus water. Experience in the Australian countries, under conditions closely resembling those in this country, points to the need of supplementing irrigation, drainage, or stump clearing by the processes of leveling and breaking the land and equipping fully the farms for use.

The Australian system of land settlement is based upon the principle that the agricultural worker deserves an even chance with the manufacturing worker, and so the farm as well as the factory should be equipped before, and not after, operations begin. Agriculture under this system is handled through the community unit as against the isolated farm unit. Not only is each farm prepared for use through initial cultivation of the soil and the erection of farm buildings but the community itself is organized for cooperative action in marketing produce, purchasing supplies, obtaining credit, and in providing for social as well as economic needs. Hence a portion of land is usually reserved at the center of each community for the location of cooperative warehouses, stores, and banks, as well as for schools and churches. At or near this center a demonstration farm may be established on which pure-bred cattle and other stock are raised and sold at cost to settlers; and this farm may be used also as a training school for incoming settlers. The opinion is growing, both in that country and in all the British countries, that the individualist type of land settlement, as practiced in "homesteading," should be supplanted by the colonization or community type which has been practiced so successfully in Australia; and the British plans for after-the-war settlement are based largely upon this colonization principle.

DEVELOPMENT OF FOREST LANDS

The permanent forest area of the United States is estimated to be 450 million acres, or nearly one-fourth the total area. Of this acreage 150 millions are contained in the Rocky Mountain and Pacific States, 90 millions are estimated as permanent farm woodlots in the Eastern States, and the remainder (210 millions) occurs throughout the mountainous and lesser settled portions of the Northeast and the Southern States, and of the Great Lakes region. About one-half of the far western forest lands are owned by the Government in national forests, and most of this land supports a virgin timber growth. The eastern forests have been cut over and very largely depleted, and are almost all in private ownership.

The Problem of "The Lumberjack"

"No one who has the interest of America at heart," says the Secretary of Labor in his latest annual report, "can look forward with tolerance to the growth or continuance of a body of migratory workers who in the nature of the case must have . . . a hatred for the law which they have never known except in its repressive aspect." [1]

The "migratory workers" here referred to are the "lumberjacks" or "timber wolves" of the forests of the Pacific Northwest. The conditions surrounding these men have received national attention during the past two years on account of the strategic industrial importance of lumber operations in the conduct of the war. These conditions were made the subject, in part, of investigations conducted in 1917 by the President's Mediation Commission, of which the Secretary of Labor was chairman. This investigation showed that about 90 per cent of the lumberjacks were unmarried and that the annual labor turnover in the lumber camps

[1] Sixth Annual Report of the Secretary of Labor (1918), pp. 221-22.

was over 600 per cent. "There has been a failure to make of these camps communities. It is not to be wondered, then, that in too many of these workers the instinct for workmanship is impaired. They are—or, rather, have been made—disintegrating forces in society." [2]

The reason why the lumber workers are migratory is because the lumber industry is migratory. Forest trees have been treated not as wood plants to be grown and cultivated, but as wood deposits to be exploited. Just as we are exhausting our mineral deposits beneath the surface, so we are exhausting our timber "deposits" above the surface. We are practicing not timber culture but "timber mining."

The ill effects of such a system upon the consuming public and the country at large have long been dwelt upon. But the inevitable effects upon the worker involved have hardly been mentioned. The lumber industry as now conducted being essentially migratory, employment therein is essentially unstable. The lumberjack must live in a camp and the man with a family is excluded as a worker. "Timber mining," being itself a tramp industry, is a breeder of tramps; it is an industry of homeless men.

Forest Community versus Logging Camp

In order that the forest industry may be put upon a basis in which the wandering "hobo" woods worker may be supplanted by the family man it will be necessary in each case that a continuous yield of timber be forthcoming yearly from an area small enough to permit of the establishment of homes on some central site to which the men can return after each day's work. The size of the forest working unit should depend, therefore, upon the facilities for transportation.

Forest operations conducted in this way would, of course, have to be planned ahead upon a long time basis, following the practice on the State-owned forests of the European countries. This might require in some cases the purchase of scattered private timber holdings within and adjacent to the national forest boundaries. One-eighth of the land within these boundaries is at present alienated and held in private ownership. Another method would be to adopt some cooperative arrangement with the owners whereby they would receive each year a part of the net returns from the whole operation, such part being in proportion to the

[2] Report of President's Mediation Commission (1918), p. 14.

amount of the timber owned by them as compared with the total amount of timber on the tract.

A typical drainage basin in the western national forests may be assumed to contain 100,000 acres of productive forest land. Suppose a series of operations be planned whereby the mature timber on this tract is to be cut off in 50 years. If the right methods of cutting are used, by the end of this 50-year period the younger trees will have grown so that the tract will be ready to be cut over again. In this way the tract can be kept continuously productive for all time. Suppose the permanent annual yield from this tract is 20,000,000 board feet. This yield would provide continuous employment for more than 150 men, who, with their families, would make a population of about 800. About half the men would be employed in the sawmill and half in the chopping operations. The sawmill, located perhaps at the entrance of the valley, would support a permanent community of about 400 people. The logging operations in the woods would support another permanent community of 400. This community would have to be relocated from time to time as different portions of the tract were being operated. But since the employment would be continuous the forest workers could at all times live in their homes with their families and maintain a community life.

Measures should be taken to see that the populations supported by the sawmill and the forest operations would develop into real communities and not mere shack towns. Aside from the maintenance of proper housing and living conditions, there are two or three fundamental community standards. These include provision for voting and self-government, for schools, churches, and educational facilities, and for cooperation among the workers to secure their economic and social welfare. It has been estimated by the United States Forest Service that the forests of the country, under a proper system of timber culture, could provide permanent employment for over 700,000 men, and thus support a population of about 3,500,000.

part two

LANDSCAPE
ARCHITECTURE
AND
PARK PLANNING

Landscape architects of the post-Civil War decades espoused a new concept of urban form—the continuous city-park-garden. Their efforts to naturalize the urban community led to the establishment of municipal park systems, new techniques of residential subdivision and design, and an enlargement of municipal planning and welfare functions. Municipal park commissions, such as the one established in Kansas City, Missouri, usually stressed the physical, psychological, and social necessity for parks in the crowded "unnatural" urban community. As this Kansas City document makes clear, however, park advocates could not justify parks on esthetic or humanitarian grounds alone. A business culture demanded an economic justification for innovations which prevented the commercial development of land. Park commissions had to demonstrate, therefore, that parks would benefit business in the long run.

At an early date, landscape architects and park commissions recognized that a large urban community had to look beyond its territorial boundaries for necessary open space. More generally, they realized that the fragmented political jurisdictions of a metropolitan area obscured the functional relationships and interdependence which existed. These points are developed in the prophetic *Report* of the Boston Metropolitan Park Commissioners, a landmark in the evolution of the metropolitan and regional planning concept. In the Boston area, the establishment of a metropolitan park district was based, in part, upon the precedent of the Metropolitan Sewerage Act of 1889.

Recommendations for the Establishment
of a Park and Boulevard System

Kansas City, Missouri

THE VALUE OF BEAUTY

Lying amidst singularly beautiful surroundings, possessing an irregular and diversified topography that would lend itself readily to improvement under the hand of the landscape architect, and abounding within her own limits in charming and, not infrequently, beautiful spots, our city has not only so far failed to make use of these advantages, but, on the contrary, the desire on the part of the owners of land to quickly bring their lands into market has resulted in destroying much of the natural beauty of our city.

There is not within the city a single reservation for public use. Localities and land that possess natural beauty of a high order, and there are many such within the city, points that command rare and distant views into and beyond the great and fertile valley of the Missouri, are in the hands of private individuals; handsome cliffs and bluffs, interesting and charming ravines, characteristic of the country about us, and which under the treatment of the skillful landscape architect would be susceptible of inexpensive conversion into most valuable public reservations, because, by preserving in them features of great natural beauty, they would, in a measure, blend the artificial structure of the city with the natural beauty of its site, and at the same time would supply recreation-grounds, are now themselves disfigured by

Report of the Board of Park and Boulevard Commissioners of Kansas City, Mo. (embracing recommendations for the establishment of a park and boulevard system for Kansas City), Resolution of October 12, 1893 (Kansas City, Mo., 1893), pp. 9-16.

shanties and worthless structures, and in turn exercise a depressing effect upon the value of adjoining lands, better suited than they for private uses.

There has been in our city thus far no public concession to esthetic considerations. We are but just beginning to realize that by beautifying our city, making our city beautiful to the eye, and a delightful place of residence, abounding in provisions that add to the enjoyment of life, we not only will do our duty to our citizens, but we shall create among our people warm attachments to the city, and promote civic pride, thereby supplementing and emphasizing our business advantages and increasing their power to draw business and population. In the location of our city, with reference to one of the largest and most prosperous agricultural sections of this country, or, for that matter, of the world, in the large number of important railways serving us, in our already large supply of important business houses, and in our banks, we possess forces that ought to, and in all probability will, make this a great commercial, manufacturing and financial place; but there are greater possibilities in store for our city. We have it in our power to make her the metropolis of that vast and fertile region, the great Southwest, which at no distant future is sure to become the home of a large and prosperous population; but to accomplish this result, we must offer more than business advantages.

To become the metropolis, that is the center, of a large and prosperous territory that contains a large population, the city must supply to a degree materially exceeding other rival cities, all the results of modern progress and of modern civilization. The city must be the center of the sum total of the thought and the activities of the people residing within the territory which the city aspires to dominate. The city must be as well the social center, if she desires to become, without successful rival, the business center.

The wholesale dry goods business has shown remarkable strength and growth within the last two years, and yet wholesale dry goods men assert that if we had one or two more wholesale hat and cap houses, one or two more clothing houses, and millinery houses, the dry goods business would thereby be much assisted. In other words, by providing additional business attraction, we would enhance the prosperity of business enterprises that we already possess.

Our Commercial Club, whose earnest and loyal efforts in behalf of the city every good citizen appreciates, has brought to our city, from time to time, people from towns and cities with which our merchants desire to trade, endeavoring, by cultivating pleasant social relations with towns and cities naturally tributary to us, to advance the business interests and to enlarge the business territory of our city. If, in addition to showing our visitors business advantages and facilities, we could in the future show a beautiful city, show in our open squares, our boulevards and parks that we pay due attention to the comfort and happiness of our people and possess rare opportunities of enjoyment, who can doubt that we would not only largely increase the respect for the enterprise of our city, but that by possessing a city head and shoulders above all cities for a great distance about us, in beauty, a city in which it would be pleasant and agreeable to live, we would add a powerful attraction that would never cease to draw our neighbors, and with them would bring their trade. Our city would then truly be the metropolis where everything is better than at home, and where many would come each year to spend some days in the enjoyment of its social and other pleasures.

The conditions of modern life make it possible for many to give great importance to advantages other than business advantages, in the choice of their permanent place of residence. A man who has been successful in the building up of a business in a small town, and after he has thoroughly organized his business, can often direct its affairs advantageously from a commercial center not too far distant, and as, with increase of wealth, his desire to enjoy life grows, he will be very apt to change his residence in favor of a beautiful city, where he can enjoy more pleasure and greater comfort than at his old home. From such men is made up the capitalist class of cities, that class to whose experience, ability and means the building up of a city is always largely due. A capitalist in the broadest sense is a man, not only of money, but possessed at the same time of business experience, sagacity and knowledge. Such men are necessarily the result of slow growth and the restricted territory of an embryo metropolis is too narrow to raise much of a crop. These men must be drawn from without. They must be furnished inducements to change their place of residence. Capital from without is hard to attract and goes always by preference into lands and buildings of a reasonably secure value. To local capital falls the task to inaugurate, promote and push new enterprises.

However, it is not only the capitalist who is attracted by the beautiful city that assures a pleasant and broad life. The same attractions have their effect upon all classes, for there is probably no man or woman that does not prefer agreeable and pleasant surroundings to the reverse, and the more intelligent and cultivated, and therefore the more productive and useful the man, the higher his demands of life. The city that confines itself to providing business advantages only, cannot in the long run, in competition with other large cities, maintain an eminent position, and certainly fails to make the fullest use of its opportunities.

THE CITY'S DUTY

The material advantage of the city, although deserving of the greatest attention and consideration, does not supply the only justification for internal improvement and beautifying. There stands out boldly the claim also of those who are not able to select their place of residence, and whose opportunity to temper the daily recurring struggle for existence with a reasonable modicum of rational enjoyment and recreation depends upon the wisdom, not less than upon the humanity, of those who influence and direct the policy of the government of a city, and of those that govern it. The duty to provide playgrounds for the children, recreation-grounds and parks for the great working body of a large city, cannot fail, and does not fail, of being admitted, and is acted upon, in every wisely governed and civilized community. To make the most of life is the highest duty of the individual, and to permit and advance its fullest development and enjoyment is clearly the first and greatest duty of every municipal corporation towards its citizens. Life in cities is an unnatural life. It has a tendency to stunt physical and moral growth. The monotony of brick and stone, of dust and dirt, the absence of the colors with which nature paints, the lack of a breath of fresh air, write despair on many a face and engrave it upon many a heart. How is the poor man's boy to grow into a cheerful, industrious and contented man, unless he can play where play alone is possible, that is, on the green turf, and under waving trees, can take with him into manhood the recollections of an innocent, joyous boyhood, instead of the impressions of dirty, white-faced and vicious gamins, and their and his acquaintance with immorality and vice.

We believe our city has reached that point where, for every reason, the undertaking of internal embellishment and the providing of playgrounds and local pleasure-grounds, or local parks, should no longer be neglected. The considerations which have been briefly sketched lead us to strongly recommend that the supplying of playgrounds and of local recreation- and pleasure-grounds should receive the first and immediate attention. We also advise that there be no delay, in at least acquiring title to parcels of land now unoccupied, or occupied by temporary structures; lands that, in addition to serving the purpose of local recreation-grounds or parks, would permit of retaining for all future time some of the characteristic features of our natural scenery, and would protect localities that possess especially fine views. There are many such opportunities in different localities of the city. The selection and improvement of such lands for public use, moreover, would make what are now drawbacks to adjacent territory, and injuriously effect the best use, and therefore the value, of adjoining property—in fact, what are now positive eyesores—elements of particular and characteristic beauty of our city. Such policy would not only make this a beautiful city, but would give the city a special character and beauty of its own.

EFFECT OF PARKWAYS OR BOULEVARDS
UPON REAL ESTATE VALUES

It is to the interest of the city, and of every individual within it, that all lands within the limits of this city be as fully and advantageously occupied as possible, and thereby become as valuable as possible. These results can be achieved only if lands are occupied and used for the purposes to which they are naturally, and therefore best, adapted, and if city improvements be so planned and carried out as to justify and encourage the fullest use and the highest possible development and improvement of all lands.

Unfortunately, the location and establishment of a city, and frequently the attainment of that dignity, are the result of pure accident. The future importance of the place, while imagined and predicted, cannot be foreseen with certainty. There is consequently a great difficulty in securing cooperation among land-owners, and a development in the general interest becomes difficult, if not impossible. Streets are laid out to accommodate either actually existing, immediate wants, as they are at the time understood and urged, or to accommodate the wishes and fancied needs of the land-owners. The laying out of additions is badly controlled, if at all, and follows the individual judgment and advantage of the land-owner, giving no heed to the advantage or the best interests of the community.

Residences go up in remote parts of the city, near the city limits, or in the suburbs, in order to escape the erratic tendency of shops and small business houses to fasten themselves upon a colony of houses that promise patronage, only, however, to draw other small shops and business houses that seem determined to capture local trade. After a period of this sort, the natural result is a large sprawling combination of city and village. A sharp division of localities, or even streets, according to use, does not exist. Uncertainty as to use is a direct hindrance to improvements, and therefore this state of affairs has encouraged the erection of temporary buildings, or of buildings of an inferior character. The conditions above described have at some period of their history been operative in most of our large cities, and have produced the same general results. Kansas City has not been an exception. With us an erratic and tantalizing topography has discouraged the adoption of a plan adapted to natural conditions and from which the best results would have been obtainable. Fifteen or twenty years ago a plan might have been adopted that would have made this one of the most beautiful cities in the world. That plan would have involved withdrawing from private use and reserving for the use of the public many of the ravines and bluffs that are but poorly suited for private improvement, but which, if improved and maintained as public reservations, would not only have laid the foundation for a magnificent park system, but would thereby have vastly increased the value of adjoining lands. It is by no means too much to say that had such a policy been pursued, the assessed valuation of lands within the limits of the city would today be far greater than it is. The difficulty at that time, however, was that such a policy could not be fully appreciated, because Kansas City was not then what she is now, and did not then promise the future that we all now believe is in store for her, and the adoption of such a policy would have seemed to involve heavy burdens upon the then smaller community. The conditions that we now actually find clearly demand that there be established, if possible, a strong tendency towards concentration and uniformity of use. A basis must be established for future development, to the end that every future improvement in the city may be of a permanent character, and of a high order. The fixing and classification of residence sections appears to be the only available remedy to correct the evils to which attention has been called. That remedy we believe will be found in the establishment of a boulevard system. Such a system, if carefully planned, if it give due weight to existing conditions and adapt itself to the topography, avoiding as much as possible forced routes and forced construction, will give a permanent residence character to certain sections of the city, and will determine and fix for a long time to come, if not permanently, the best and most valuable residence property. It will do more. By giving within the city some of the advantages of the country, but better roads and better kept roads than are usually found in the suburbs, in addition to all the advantages that city life affords, a comprehensive, well-planned and thoroughly maintained system of boulevards will check the tendency to spread out and to build residences in the suburbs, by producing the opposite tendency, that is, to build within the city.

The checking of the tendency to spread out and to build up suburbs, and thereby bringing about the more complete utilization of lands, and the close building up, within the city, is, under proper conditions, not only no disadvantage, but an advantage, because it will encourage the most complete sanitary provisions and the best maintenance of streets and alleys. Even street car companies are benefited by checking the tendency to build up suburbs, for a line through a well-settled section within the city yields much greater revenue than a long suburban line.

The best and most expensive residences will go up along boulevards, but these avenues will exercise a decided effect upon the character of residences to a considerable distance on each side. They will, in fact, create compactly and well built-up residence sections.

The residence sections firmly established, retail business that supplies the many and frequent wants of the family will find its legitimate foothold, and all buildings erected for the purposes of such business will conform to the character of the improvements along the street and in the section on and in which they are located, thereby further adding to, instead of detracting from, the general harmony and uniformity of improvements and helping to establish the same more firmly. The general retail business will develop a strong tendency towards concentration upon certain streets most advantageously situated, thereby bringing about a more compact building-up of such streets. The occupation of lands generally within the city will be encouraged and will henceforth be in accord with the uses to which these lands are best adapted. Values of lands within the city will reach a level in harmony with the uses to which the lands are best suited, and those uses having been definitely established, values, instead of being variable and uncertain, will become fixed. The condition where blacksmith shop, hotel, store and residence dwell peacefully side by side is the condition of the village. In the city the retail merchant will select, as the most advantageous location, the street that contains many establishments of the same character as his. The man desiring to build a handsome residence will expect to be able to select a street which is sure to be used for residence purposes only, and for residences of the same class as that which he intends to build. It is such uniformity of use in a restricted territory that gives special value to lands.

EXPERIENCE OF OTHER CITIES

The experience of other large cities that have undertaken systematic park and boulevard construction is in complete harmony with the conclusions presented above. The experience of Chicago is especially interesting, because its boulevard and park improvements are entirely artificial. Chicago possessed no diversified topography, had no lands or places of a high order of natural beauty, no well-wooded sections that possessed really good trees, to invite utilization for pleasure-grounds or drives, and still, under these discouraging conditions there has been created, by purely artificial means, though with the employment of the very highest skill, a beautiful and gigantic system of boulevards and parks, which admittedly has been of great advantage to Chicago. Chicago and her parks and boulevards are mentioned in the same breath. Without her parks and boulevards Chicago would not be the city she is today; would not possess the tremendous power of attracting men and money that has enabled her to assume, within a few years, her place among the great cities of the world, and that has enabled her to plan and successfully execute some of the most gigantic enterprises the world has ever known. A careful observer of Chicago's park and boulevard system cannot fail to notice the illustration, on a grand scale, of the effect of boulevards upon the full utilization of lands within the city, and upon the sharp separation of localities as to use. Towards the south, which is the principal direction in which boulevards and parks have been constructed, the vacant lands between former suburbs, such as Hyde Park, and the main city, are rapidly filling up with first-class residences. There is not a boulevard in Chicago, in any direction, that does not show in a marked degree and manner its influence upon the character of the buildings upon its sides. So well is this influence appreciated in Chicago, that, even with her already tremendous system, plans for new and additional construction are constantly under consideration, and even now are in process of execution. On Grand Boulevard residence property sells at $500.00 a foot, and on the handsomer Drexel Boulevard values reach $1,000.00 per foot. The business sections are sharply defined and closely built up. The following list of Chicago boulevards and parks, which has not been revised for some years, will give an idea of the importance and significance of this class of city improvement in our successful and prosperous neighbor.

SOUTH PARK DISTRICT

Boulevards	Length	Width
Michigan Avenue Boulevard	5¾ miles	100 feet
Drexel Boulevard	1½ "	200 "
Grand Boulevard	2 "	198 "
Oakwood Boulevard	½ "	100 "
Garfield Boulevard	3.5 "	200 "
Western Avenue Boulevard	2.81 "	200 "
Thirty-fifth Street Boulevard	.32 "	— "
Fifty-seventh Street Boulevard	.03 "	100 "

Total mileage of boulevards, 16.37, of which considerably over one-half, namely, 9.89 miles, have a width of 200 feet.

Regional Planning

Boston Metropolitan Park Commissioners

NEED OF AMPLE PROVISION OF OPEN SPACES, AND DIFFICULTIES IN THE WAY OF OBTAINING THEM

GENTLEMEN: The provision of ample open spaces for public recreation and the promotion of public health is now universally regarded as an essential feature in the proper equipment of urban communities. In all parts of the civilized world the leading cities are recognizing this necessity. The younger cities are perceiving the wisdom of providing amply for the future in this respect by securing lands in suitable locations and in sufficient amount, to be developed with the growth of their population. The older cities, like London, Paris and Berlin, though long possessed of extensive reservations of this description, are today finding their amount of open spaces inadequate, and are taking measures for securing extensive areas in addition that will meet the needs of the future.

It was in view of the needs of the country around Boston that the General Court of 1892 authorized the appointment of a commission to investigate the subject, directing that a plan be reported for providing ample open spaces for the use of the public in the towns and cities in the vicinity of Boston.

1. Some Contradictory Aspects of the Metropolitan Region

A stranger looking over the country lying within ten or twelve miles of the Boston city hall, and ignorant of the existence of the po-

Report of the Board of Metropolitan Park Commissioners (Boston, January, 1893), pp. 1-4, 9-10.

litical boundaries separating, by almost wholly "imaginary lines," the various cities and towns that make up one of the densest masses of population to be found in the new world upon an area of like extent, would be puzzled to account for certain things that could not fail to attract his attention. He would see what appeared to be one great city massed around the shores of the harbor and along the banks of the rivers emptying therein, its thousands of buildings spreading irregularly out into the valleys and over the hill slopes of the surrounding country. He would see this great city occupying a region of remarkable and diversified landscape interest; a bay with beautiful shores and numerous islands large and small, a country varied with hills and fields, wood-land, meadows, lakes and streams. He would find the population comprised within a considerable segment of the southerly half of this region provided with extensive facilities for public open-air recreation; an admirably devised system of parks, parkways and boulevards, public gardens and playgrounds, forming continuous chains of pleasure ground, or sprinkled liberally over the territory. Throughout the rest of the great urban area, with few exceptions, he would see almost nothing of the kind. He would behold miles and miles of thickly settled territory, with practically not a square yard of public ground. He would naturally wish to know the reason for this remarkable contrast; why a certain portion of the population should be so favored, while the other portions were entirely without the needed facilities? Wherefore luxury and abundance on one side, and beyond the opposite? He would be informed that the reason was that the favored portion of the population formed one municipality by itself, and by the concentration of its wealth and energy thus made possible had been enabled to provide for its own needs; while the rest of the population—comprising nearly one-half of the entire number of inhabitants occupying the region, and from its rate of growth soon destined to comprise much the larger part of the whole—being split up into various small communities, divided upon political and not natural lines, had been unable to provide for its needs in an intelligent manner, and thus was in danger of becoming a vast desert of houses, factories and stores, spreading over and overwhelming the natural features of the landscape, as lines of sand dunes, advancing from the seashore, overwhelm and obliterate the woods and fields. The creation of such a human desert, relieved by hardly an oasis, is threatened upon the greater part of this naturally beautiful region.

2. Peculiar Political Geography of the Neighborhood of Boston

The exceptional nature of this densely populated and rapidly growing section of the Commonwealth now generally known as the "metropolitan district of Boston" is therefore seen to be such as to demand a peculiar method of treatment, under legislation framed especially for the purpose. The excellent legislative provisions that have from time to time been made to meet the necessities of the various communities of the Commonwealth in the way of parks and other open spaces for recreative purposes cannot with good results be applied to the requirements of this region. With few exceptions, the other cities and towns of the State are each clearly defined social, as well as political, entities. Each can therefore be safely left to look out for itself in all the varied concerns that make up the wants of a modern community. The State has but to grant the necessary authority, has but to provide the machinery adapted to the exercise of the respective functions, and each community can then be trusted to meet its own needs as they arise.

Quite different is it with the Boston metropolitan district. While divided by political lines into a large number of cities and towns, socially this district is, to all intents and purposes, essentially one community. It must therefore be considered such when questions present themselves arising from the needs developed by the growth of such a community. For, if the various cities and towns forming this great urban composite are in the future, as they have been in the past, to be treated separately, these needs can be met only in the most unsatisfactory manner, and in a way that cannot fail to impede the healthy growth and hamper the proper development which should characterize a community of this class.

It is evident that the political conformation and organization of a community should be governed by its physical character. When, at or near its foundation, an important city is planned with foresight, when the direction which its future growth is to take becomes clearly evident, we may see this exemplified. Cases in point are large cities in the West, like Chicago and Minneapolis, where with wise forethought all the territory that appears needful for the natural expansion of those cities has been brought under one jurisdiction; not with the purpose, as has been asserted, of figuring up a great area and population, but in order that the demands of the future may be met in the best possible manner as they may arise, and without waste of energy and money. Our national capital is one of the best instances of a great city planned with a view to its growth into what it has now become, and it is consequently easier to provide it with the equipment necessary for a modern municipality than almost any other centre of population.

The development of the great metropolitan population in and about the present city of Boston has proceeded in a quite different manner. A glance at the map is sufficient to show us how it is cut up by local community boundary lines, not only without the least regard to the physical character of the region, but almost, it would seem, in wilful disregard of such character.

•   •   •

5. Various Needs That Require Consideration

This problem is also largely one of sanitation, but having the wider scope of promoting the physical and moral health of the community. Nothing appears to be better settled than the fact that a population living under urban conditions, amidst the incessant activity, the noise, the confusion and the excitement incident to city life, must, for the maintenance of its health and the perpetuation of desirable types of humanity, be afforded frequent opportunities for the relaxation of the strain which these conditions of life impose; and these opportunities are best found in the means of escape into more natural and agreeable surroundings.

Thereto must be added the requirements of the growing generations in the shape of ample playground facilities, situated within convenient distances of their homes, where sport and exercise in the open air may be obtained, developing the body and quickening the senses, while removing children from other modes of amusement, most detrimental physically and morally. Without resources of this kind the suburban movement of population, which has been hailed as presenting a complete solution to the tenement-house and other crying evils common to a dense population, would by no means prove the blessing anticipated. In fact, it would furnish only a very temporary benefit.

Through lack of foresight in this direction there are already, as we have seen, well settled expanses of suburban population, with acres and acres of streets and houses where a few years ago were pastures and woodland, possessing no open spaces whatever; not a square foot of public ground outside of schoolhouse yards and streets belonging to the cities and towns in question.

A few years, sooner or later, will witness all these suburban tracts completely urbanized; and, unless something is done in the near future, the only alternative to the perpetuation of a most unhealthy condition for these districts will be the clearing away, at enormous cost, of sufficient open spaces here and there to furnish local playgrounds, as is now being done in New York and London.

Preferable to a suburban development of this kind, such as the now rapidly increasing provision of transportation facilities in every direction is causing, without a corresponding provision for open spaces to meet the needs of this movement of population, would seem a concentration upon compact areas covered with dwellings such as modern science and art can devise, surrounding small squares or large courtyards that would supply playgrounds combined with pleasant gardens. However, the movement of population suburbanwards can be made all that is claimed for it by providing in time the needed breathing spaces, parks and playgrounds.

A third aspect of the problem is one which is more strictly sanitative in character, and is furnished by the present conditions of the streams and other water spaces, to prevent the pollution of which prompt attention and treatment is demanded. It would seem that the simplest, cheapest, and most effective method of dealing with this problem, and therefore the most practical, is furnished by combining therewith the recreative purposes which a stream and its shores can usually be made to serve in most abundant measure.

•　　•　　•

part three

HOUSING REFORM:
RESTRICTIVE
LEGISLATION

American housing reform, beginning in the nineteenth century, focused almost exclusively upon the sanitary and social pathology of the urban slum. Housing reformers maintained that substandard dwellings not only nurtured the cycle of disease and poverty, but also contributed to family and social demoralization. In this sense, housing betterment was an instrument of social control in the urban community. The following selection attempts to explain why the unreformed tenement slum undermined citizenship and civic responsibility.

Lawrence Veiller (1872-1959), author of this influential housing handbook, dominated American housing reform between 1900 and World War I. He introduced a degree of centralization and technical proficiency which had not previously existed. Most city and state housing codes prior to the 1920's were based upon the New York State Tenement House Law of 1901 which Veiller authored, or his "model" housing laws published by the Russell Sage Foundation. As founder and secretary of the National Housing Association, he advised housing groups throughout the nation.

By later standards, Veiller's approach to housing betterment was conservative. It centered almost exclusively upon restrictive legislation —codes affecting structural and sanitary standards. He vehemently opposed government subsidy of any kind, although restrictive legislation could only prevent the worst housing from being built. It could not insure an adequate supply of good housing at rents or costs which low-income groups could afford.

restriction not subsidies

Housing Evils and Their Significance

Lawrence Veiller

Every American city has its housing problem. While in no two cities the same, in all there are certain underlying conditions which find common expression. Bad housing conditions generally first manifest themselves when several families are found living in a dwelling intended originally for a single family. Then, with the increase in population, there comes the building of regular tenement houses usually before any restrictions have been thought of by the community. Rapidly from this point develop the evils of cellar dwellings, unsanitary privies, lack of drainage, inadequate water supply, filthy out-premises, defective plumbing, dark rooms and halls, overcrowding, the taking in of lodgers, congestion, excessive rents, the sweating evil and those other manifestations of modern social life which are too often seen in our large cities.

The causes for these evils are not to be found in any one thing but are to be traced through a variety of influences operating through considerable periods of time. Some of the evils are peculiar to a single community, but most of them sooner or later are found in all cities. The chief underlying factor which stands out in every community is that they are, in nearly every case, due to neglect and ignorance. Neglect on the part of the community, failure of its citizens to recognize evil tendencies as they develop; dangerous ignorance on the part of citizens and public officials of what is going on within the city's gates —a feeling of safety and of confidence that all must be right because

Lawrence Veiller, *Housing Reform: A Hand-Book for Practical Use in American Cities* (New York: Russell Sage Foundation, 1910), pp. 3-7.

they see little that is wrong, that things cannot be bad as long as they are hidden; a false civic pride which believes that everything in one's own city is the best, a dangerous sort of apathy content to leave things as they are, a *laissez faire* policy which brings forth fruit of unrighteousness.

Invariably accompanying these two causes, but to a lesser degree, is found a third, greed. Greed on the part of those persons who for the sake of a larger profit on their investments, are willing to traffic in human lives, to sacrifice the health and welfare of countless thousands.

It is only in comparatively recent years that the community as a whole has been alive to the importance of right housing conditions, and the far-reaching influence of wrong ones. With the changed view that has come of late with regard to much of our modern charitable and social effort, emphasis has come to be placed more and more upon the environment in which people live, and less upon those hereditary traits of character which social workers of earlier years were wont to observe.

It is not so very many years since we were told that it was practically useless to attempt to improve the condition of the poor; that their poverty was caused by their own vices, by defects of character transmitted from father to son, from generation to generation, by faults which were in the blood, hereditary traits and instincts impossible to overcome. The theory that tuberculosis was an incurable hereditary disease prevailed with equal force about the same period. We know now, however, that both these views were erroneous; that poverty, too, is a germ disease, contagious even at times; that it thrives amid the same conditions as those under which the germs of tuberculosis flourish —in darkness, filth and sordid surroundings; and that when the light has once been let in the first step towards its cure has been taken.

Environment leaves its ineffaceable records on the souls, minds and bodies of men, there to be read by all able to understand. A child living its early years in dark rooms, without sunlight or fresh air, does not grow up to be a normal healthy person, but is anaemic, weak, sickly, like a plant grown in the dark. He is handicapped in his school life; his earning capacity is diminished and his resisting power weakened. It is not of such material that strong nations are made. Improvement of social conditions, as indeed of all others, starts with the improvement of domestic life. When there are no homes there will be no nation.

While every American city has its housing problem, fortunately but few cities have as yet a tenement house problem. The two are quite distinct and should be carefully differentiated. Moreover, no city in America, except New York, need have a tenement house problem. The few that have can easily solve their problems at their present stage of development, if they will be active and vigilant.

It should be recognized at the outset that the normal method of housing the working population in our American cities is in small houses, each house occupied by a separate family, often with a small bit of land, with privacy for all, and with a secure sense of individuality and opportunity for real domestic life. Under no other method can we expect American institutions to be maintained. It is useless to expect a conservative point of view in the workingman, if his home is but three or four rooms in some huge building in which dwell from twenty to thirty other families, and this home is his only from month to month. Where a man has a home of his own he has every incentive to be economical and thrifty, to take his part in the duties of citizenship, to be a real sharer in government. Democracy was not predicated upon a country made up of tenement dwellers, nor can it so survive.

It is in such small houses that the great mass of the working people are housed in most of our cities. It is so in Philadelphia, Chicago, Boston, Detroit, Baltimore, Washington, Pittsburgh, St. Louis, Cincinnati, Buffalo, Cleveland, Indianapolis, San Francisco, St. Paul, Minneapolis, and in fact in all the larger cities except New York. In many of these cities, however, several families live in one building, in some cities there are frequently two families to a house, in others three, and in others even more. In a few, the tenement house system has begun to develop; and in all of those mentioned there are found individual tenement houses, similar to those of New York—large buildings four or five stories high, with several families on each floor, and with all the usual features of the multiple dwelling. But in none of these cities, as yet, has this become the dominant type of building. In that lies the hopeful element of the situation.

Home strengthens democracy & conser.
Urban yeoman idea

part four

THE
CITY
BEAUTIFUL

The City Beautiful movement espoused the ideal of the city as a work of art. It aspired, through planning, to universalize the beauty Americans had briefly glimpsed at the Chicago World's Fair of 1893 and at subsequent Fairs. John Brisben Walker (editor of *Cosmopolitan Magazine*) outlines the new urban vision, which stimulated the preparation of numerous city plans in the early twentieth century. Walker makes it apparent that the defects of the City Beautiful idea were balanced, in part, by its singular educational achievement. The City Beautiful aroused a mood of dissatisfaction with existing cities, which in the long run encouraged planning and beautification efforts. Walker's references to homes and factories and to the general interest of City Beautiful planners in park and street systems imply a greater interest in utilitarian issues than some critics of the City Beautiful have recognized. It is clear, however, from Walker's article, that the City Beautiful did suffer from a static conception of planning, one which stressed "harmony" and order rather than adaptation and change.

Daniel H. Burnham, the distinguished Chicago architect, prepared his San Francisco plan at the request of the Association for the Improvement and Adornment of San Francisco. The selection illustrates the great emphasis of City Beautiful planners upon the improvement of street systems and the creation of civic centers. With less skillful management than Burnham's, the City Beautiful might degenerate into a scheme for superficial municipal embellishment, pivoting around an elephantine civic center and the slicing of great diagonal boulevards.

The City of the Future: A Prophecy

John Brisben Walker

One cannot enter the gates of the Pan-American Exposition at Buffalo—that wonder of color and form which rises before the visitor —without mentally reverting to the City of White Palaces of 1893, only eight years ago, with its throngs of amazed and delighted people. Even while the mind is filled with delight and astonishment, there comes a subconscious picture of the neglected "Pinta" which sailed so boldly across the Atlantic, and now lies abandoned in a marsh from which rise the charred ends of many piles—the only remaining vestiges of that famous White City. What a shame if these marvelous creations at Buffalo are to meet a similar fate! "What a pity," the visitor reflects, "that another two or three millions could not have been added to the funds at the disposal of the commission, and the walls stand in substantial brick and mortar instead of wood and staff!" It might have required that the Exposition should have been located a few miles farther out on the prairie. Then at its close the aggregation of palaces might have been converted into a model city; the Palace of Liberal Arts become a great factory; the Temple of Music stand as the theater hall; the Stadium remain the great amphitheater that it is, to which Buffalo could flock in years to come for its amusement. Games would, doubtless, be born worthy of the dignity of their surroundings. The buildings constructed by the states of North and South America would become private houses set in the most beautiful of parks. Probably three-fourths of the cost of the Exposition has been in the work on its designing, its

John Brisben Walker, "The City of the Future: A Prophecy," *The Cosmopolitan,* **31** (May-October, 1901), 473-75.

parks, its waterways, and the workmanship of its architecture and monuments. Only the materials of the exterior are temporary. Another million or, at the most, two millions expended would have left every wall in the most durable of materials. What a pity then, what a waste that this small additional sum should not have left the work of great artists in lasting form!

For this is the lesson of the fair—that it illustrates what men working in harmonious effort may accomplish for the delight of all. Who believes that the people of the second half of our new century will be content to live in those abominations of desolation which we call our great cities—brick and mortar piled higgledy-piggledy, glaringly vulgar, stupidly offensive, insolently trespassing on the right to sunshine and fresh air, conglomerate result of a competitive individualism which takes no regard for the rights of one's neighbor?

Wandering in these streets of varied forms, the mind is entranced by the eternally changing color always in marvelous harmony. Down the great central court to the left, by the fountains on the Esplanade, in the maze of the Horticultural and the Graphic Arts Buildings, then under the graceful pergolas to the magnificent erections on the Bridge of Triumph, the colors change and change until the whole prismatic spectrum seems to have been exhausted twenty times over—yet never a repetition, only restful harmony.

How was this marvel of construction brought about? Why three miles away are a thousand ungraceful shapes piled garishly together, and here this dream of perfection? The answer comes—it is but the difference in systems. One represents human effort disastrously expended under individual guidance in the competitive system which takes no thought of neighbor. The other represents organization intended for the best enjoyment of all. One stands as the remnant of a barbarism handed down through the centuries. The other stands for the aspiration of the human mind under the unfolding intelligence of an advancing civilization. In the light of this new city the old seems almost as much of an anachronism as the walled city of the Middle Ages with its turrets and donjon and drawbridge and portcullis.

How was this present marvel constructed? Very simply. The men of high intelligence whose liberality is responsible for this exhibit came together and said: "Let us seek out the great artists in architecture, in sculpture, in landscape, and bring them here to Buffalo. Then we will ask them to work out in unison a scheme, every part of which shall be in perfect harmony with every other part; shape, environment, distance, color, shall all unite in one great harmony."

The Chinese philosophers have derived from their four thousand years of study one idea of heaven, and their word for it is *harmony*. Through all their highest philosophical ideals runs this one word— harmony. With their limited economic conditions they have never been able to express this conception in material form. It has been left for this richest of peoples twice to make expression of it in form and color. This, then, may be taken as the great central idea of the Pan-American Exposition—a Prophecy of what the city of the future must be—a beautiful location arranged, first, with reference to its landscape; second, with reference to its form and perfection, and, next, with reference to satisfying the eye in its blending colors—all carefully planned and worked out with reference to the uses to which it is to be put.

When commerce ceases to be war, when the world ceases to educate its best brains for the destruction which is meant by competition, when human talent shall be converted to its highest sphere of usefulness, then we shall have the sites of cities selected by commissions having the highest good of the proposed community at heart, instead of by cornerers and peddlers of real estate.

Sanitary advantage will be considered in a scientific way, and homes and factories will be outlined with reference to the highest advantage of the entire community. Harmony throughout all will be sought, instead of the freaks of individuality.

Report on a Plan for San Francisco

Daniel H. Burnham

THE PROBLEM

It is proposed to make a comprehensive plan of San Francisco, based upon the present streets, parks and other public places and grounds, which shall interfere as little as possible with the rectangular street system of the city.

Scope

The scope of this report is general. It covers such subjects as the direction and length of all the proposed streets, parkways and boulevards; the size and location of proposed *Places*, round points and playgrounds; the size, location and broad treatment of proposed parks; and closes with general recommendations. It is not the province of a report of this kind to indicate the exact details very closely.

It is not to be supposed that all the work indicated can or ought to be carried out at once, or even in the near future. A plan beautiful and comprehensive enough for San Francisco can only be executed by degrees, as the growth of the community demands and as its financial ability allows.

The plan is so devised that the execution of each part will contribute to the final result. That result will combine convenience and beauty in the greatest possible degree.

Daniel H. Burnham, assisted by Edward H. Bennett, *Report on a Plan for San Francisco* (San Francisco, 1905), pp. 35-36, 39-44.

A scheme of parks, streets and public grounds for a city, in order to be at once comprehensive and practical, should take into account the public purse of today and embrace those things that can be immediately carried into effect, but should in no wise limit itself to these. It should be designed not only for the present, but for all time to come.

While prudence holds up a warning finger, we must not forget what San Francisco has become in 50 years and what it is still further destined to become. Population and wealth are rapidly increasing, culture is advancing. The city looks toward a sure future wherein it will possess in inhabitants and money many times what it has now. It follows that we must not found the scheme on what the city is, so much as on what it is to be. We must remember that a meager plan will fall short of perfect achievement, while a great one will yield large results, even if it is never fully realized.

Our purpose, therefore, must be to stop at no line within the limits of practicability. Our scope must embrace the possibilities of development of the next 50 years.

A city plan must ever deal mainly with the direction and width of its streets. The streets of San Francisco are laid out at right angles and with little regard for grades and other physical difficulties. It may be impossible to overcome all the embarrassments arising from this condition, but certainly we can lessen them materially.

The difficulty may largely be conquered by girdling the city with a boulevard—a method of facilitating communication which is by no means new. To this embracing highway all streets lead, and access may be had from any one of them to another lying in a distant section by going out to this engirdling boulevard and following it until the street sought opens into it. This method of communication, enabling one to avoid the congested districts, is a delightful one, although not so direct and useful as the diagonal streets within the city, which will be particularly described hereafter.

This boulevard should be a broad, dignified and continuous driveway skirting the water edge and passing completely around the city. There are several streets and parkways already in use that may become parts of it; the others should be undertaken at an early date, because there is no work to be done on the thoroughfares of San Francisco that will yield greater immediate and lasting results.

To open all the diagonal streets proposed in the plan will be the work of a generation, as was the case in Paris, but once the outer encircling driveway is established, these diagonals will follow, affording direct and satisfactory access to it from the various centers.

GENERAL THEORY OF THE CITY

A study of the cities of the Old World develops the fact that the finest examples—Paris, Berlin, Vienna, Moscow and London—consist of a number of concentric rings separated by boulevards. The smallest of these rings, inclosing the Civic Center—that portion of the city which plays the most important part in civic life—is located at or near the geographical center.

The Perimeter of Distribution

From this inner circuit boulevard, run diagonal arteries to every section of the city and far into the surrounding country. Intersecting in the first place the periphery, or outer wall, they traverse in succession the various circuit boulevards, which represent in themselves the successive stages of the city's growth, and finally reach the center or group of centers which, in a measure, they traverse to connect with one another and form continuous arteries from one side of the city to the other.

It is on this study that the proposed system of circulation for a larger and greater San Francisco is based. Experience shows that the radial arteries should be many, and that the inner circuit from which they start should be small in radius. This circuit has been named the perimeter of distribution. It surrounds the center which the radial arteries traverse (which may be termed the center of circulation), and in conjunction with this it forms the Civic Center.

The Civic Center

In a city as large as San Francisco is destined to be, no central *Place* will be adequate for the grouping of the public buildings. The Civic Center will, therefore, develop around the center in the form of a number of sub-centers having for location the intersection of the radial arteries with the perimeter of distribution. At each of these intersections there should be a public *Place*.

Unlike the cities above mentioned, whose communications with the surrounding country are evenly divided among their radial arteries, San Francisco, situated as it is at the extremity of a peninsula, has a waterfront for its periphery on three sides. The eastern shore receives supplies from the surrounding country by water, and communicates with the center by means of radial arteries, just as the northern and western sections do. Once the western section is built up, however, the city can develop only in one direction—toward the south, and as far as land communication goes, has but three arteries for supplies from the southern country and for circulation from the city to the suburbs and the country beyond.

Mission Boulevard

Of these the most important artery will be, must be, the proposed Mission Boulevard and its continuation, the Camino Real, the backbone of development to the south. It is proposed that this shall reach the Civic Center as directly as possible (which it does, as shown on the plan, by passing through the future center of the Mission), and to build it of dimensions corresponding to its future importance. This is readily seen by a comparison with the radial arteries to the country of the above mentioned cities, for which it is virtually the unique substitute.

Relation of the Civic Center
to the Financial and Manufacturing Districts

The Civic Center thus described is one of administration, education, amusement and shopping of the finer order. There are two other sections of the city which may be regarded as centers—the financial district, in the vicinity of California and Sansome Streets, and the manufacturing district, south of Market Street. These are closely related to each other and to the Civic Center. They communicate with the Civic Center, the former by means of Market Street, the latter by the Panhandle extension south of Market.

San Francisco can possess the innermost and outermost boulevards mentioned above. The former is the perimeter of distribution; the latter, the periphery, can easily be developed as a boulevard. But the intermediary circuit boulevards, if carried in a concentric form, would be impracticable, owing to the hills. They are therefore replaced, as suggested in the plan, by a series of contour roads circumscribing the hills, connected with each other on the level ground by arteries (for the most part parkways), with which they form an irregular chain concentric to the inner perimeter, as complete as the topography will allow.

ELEMENTS OF THE CITY—ADMINISTRATIVE AND EDUCATIONAL

The city may be divided into the following elements: (1) administrative and educational, (2) economical, (3) residential.

(1) This is the real being of the city proper; all else should contribute to its honor and maintenance. In its national character it guarantees the city's relation to the country and in its civic character to the citizens.

This center comprises:

First, those structures devoted to the interests of matters administrative, of national, municipal, judicial and educational character, grouped in proper relation to one another:

City Hall
Court of Justice
Custom House
Appraisers' Building
State Building
U.S. Government Building and Postoffice

Second, those structures, public or private, of monumental character and of great civic interest relating to matters literary, musical, esthetic, expositional, professional or religious:

Library
Opera House
Concert Hall
Municipal Theater
Academy of Art
Technical and Industrial School
Museum of Art

Museum of Natural History
Academy of Music
Exhibition Hall
Assembly Hall

These buildings, composed in esthetic and economic relation, should face on the avenue forming the perimeter of distribution, and on the radial arteries within, and in particular on the public *Places* formed by their intersection and should have on all sides extensive settings contributing to public rest and recreation and adapted to celebrations, fetes, etc.

Both groups, relating directly to the spacious *Place*, the heart of the city's circulation, and removed from the direct flow and press of business, will gain in repose and strengthen the public sense of the dignity and responsibility of citizenship.

A grand vestibule to the city should be placed on the chief radial line from this *Place*. This will be the Union Railway Station.

That some elements of the Civic Center thus formed should constitute in themselves a separate group:

Postoffice
Custom House
Court House
Appraisers' Building, etc.

may be expedient or desirable, if not imperative. It should, however, be in as direct communication as possible with the administrative group.

It is desirable that theaters and places of amusement be grouped on some one large artery near the center, with ample space for the crowd of spectators going and coming.

ELEMENTS OF THE CITY—ECONOMICAL

(2) The economical element of the city involves two considerations: (a) distribution, (b) finance.

(a) Distribution. This includes international and internal commerce and comprises:

Wholesale trade
Retail trade

Manufactures
Dockage and Wharves
The Railroad Depot

The freight depots, docks, and wharves group naturally on the waterfront. They should be planned for indefinite expansion and connected with a complete system of warehouses—served on the one hand by railroad tracks or canals and on the other by broad roadways. The warehouse system should be so schemed as to distribute the raw material directly to the manufacturing quarter, and other products as directly as possible to the wholesale trade districts. These in their turn must distribute easily to the retail quarter. The retail quarter follows, in general, in its growth, the residential districts which it serves, limited by the steeper grades of the contours. Thus the whole working city is governed in its location and growth by the two conditions of a maritime city—the waterfront and the available level ground.

Waterfront

San Francisco possesses about ten miles of waterfront. As compared with other large cities this is very little, and there is no doubt that it will be inadequate to the needs of the future. Although there is nothing to check its expansion down the eastern bay shore to the county line and beyond, its value decreases as it becomes more remote from the center of the city. It is therefore thought necessary to develop as much as possible that part of the waterfront extending from the ferries to Hunter's Point. A system of docks, inclosed by the sea wall, as shown on the plan, would triple or even quadruple the extent of wharfage. The increased quantities of cargo would be stored in a system of extensive warehouses, thus concentrating shipping as much as possible. It is not the aim here to solve the problem of property interests or to lay down in detail the scheme suggested, but merely to indicate the direction in which it should be studied. The question of circulation to and from the city has been considered and will explain itself.

The Outer Boulevard follows the sea wall. It is necessary to connect it with that section of the city lying near it, inhabited by people of moderate means. Where the main arteries from this section intersect it, there should be piers for public recreation, a yacht and boat harbor and vast bathing places, both inclosed and open-air. People will seek the

Outer Boulevard, and will find refreshment and benefit from the water frontage. The design of the roadway arranges for this without interfering with its use for shipping.

Subways

Rapid underground transit solves the problem of moving large crowds from one center to another in a manner that no surface system can accomplish, and inasmuch as surface traction renders boulevards less agreeable and less serviceable for other traffic, it is suggested that the main diagonal arteries proposed on the plan should be provided with an underground service of cars traversing the center by means of a loop described under the central plaza (the necessary excavations made simultaneously with the construction of the new arteries). There should be another loop line under the artery described as perimeter of distribution. At least two lines should be constructed at right angles to one another as the growth of the population warrants; the most pressing need at the present is that of Market Street. The economy in time of covering the greater part of a journey across town, by rapid transit, completing it by transfer with a surface car, is self-evident. The problem in its simple form, on level ground or slight grades, has been dealt with successfully in other cities and needs no comment. Where, however, the steeper grades and contour roadways extending around the hills are encountered, it is suggested that the subway might be built as a gallery, below the roadway, opening to the view, or the car line built on the slope slightly below the roadway.

The wholesale quarter represents:

1. Natural Products
2. Manufactures

The former should be given precedence in accessibility to the retail dealers and markets for the daily distribution of perishable goods.

When necessary the retail quarter should be relieved from congestion by arcades and should have broad sidewalks.

(b) Finance. The finance center comprises: Banks, exchanges, insurance buildings, and general office structures. It is most naturally situated between the wholesale and retail quarters, should be directly accessible to these from at least one great artery of the city and also from the administrative center.

The ideal would be, perhaps, a financial forum, which although surrounded and served by working roadways, should exclude vehicles from its center. In the form of a court or series of courts it should be fronted by the most important and frequented financial concerns; the Stock Exchange placed as the focal point on the main axis.

ELEMENTS OF THE CITY—RESIDENTIAL

(3) Residential: (a) urban, (b) suburban, (c) country.

(a) The residential districts develop as necessity demands; the pioneers or small households retiring in many districts before the advance of better improvements. The most desirable district should be studied in anticipation for the right size of block, size of street and general disposition, preservation of view points, park areas, etc., in order that once settled into place the best districts may be valuable to all and initial errors will not have to be rectified at great cost. A great charm might be lent to certain quarters, particularly the less expensive and flatter sections of the city, by the elimination of some of the streets in the monotonous system of blocks, and substitution of a chain of park-like squares, formed in a measure by the unused or misused back-yard areas.

The isolated square of the Old World, unless maintained by wealthy residents, is a quiet, almost desolate spot, seldom feeling the throb of life. The chain is suggested to obviate this, and induce a current of life to flow agreeably from end to end, to the exclusion of unnecessary vehicles, thus leaving the main traffic to the intermediate streets. In case the houses front on the squares a new system might be evolved. Thus the cars and service might be thrown on the streets (narrowed), whilst the Park chains would become public avenues of beautiful planting, in which one could walk with great comfort, and where children could play, free from danger of traffic. Such a system would provide well for children who seldom know any life except that upon the streets of the city and would be the natural approach or connecting link between the larger parks and the playgrounds.

Borough Centers

As the city grows such places as Colma, Ocean View and Baden, which will eventually become borough centers, should reserve large commons, on which may face the civic buildings.

Theory of the Hills

Theoretically the hills are a series of planes diminishing in their ascent. Considering only the more important hills, this indicates the character which should be given to roads climbing them, for each hill or succession of hills should be circumscribed at its base, as already described, by a circuit road. As the higher levels are reached in unbuilt tracts the level circuits or contour roads become easy of accomplishment. They should be repeated at various heights and should be connected by easy inclines. Places of interest should be emphasized by terraces with appropriate approaches.

part five

THE
GARDEN
CITY

The Garden City was among the most radical urban reform movements. It proposed a new orientation to urban growth, based upon limits on the size of cities, and growth by nucleation (the creation of new cities) rather than indefinite expansion of existing centers. Planned industrial and residential suburbs, described by Howe, were often confused with the Garden City. The latter implied a combination of residential and employment opportunities, and diverse civic facilities. All three community types, however, popularized the idea of planned urban decentralization as a basis for improving housing and living conditions. A major source of their appeal was the opportunity they presented to restore man to the land. Indeed, Ebenezer Howard had described the Garden City as a "magnet" which combined the advantages of town and country, but eliminated the existing disadvantages of each.

A disciple of Tom Johnson, Cleveland's reform mayor in the early twentieth century, Howe published many books and articles on municipal affairs. He was greatly impressed by the management of European cities, particularly German and English. Howe attributed their superiority to administration by experts, and to the unhesitant use of government power to promote the general welfare.

The Garden Cities of England

Frederic C. Howe

Belated transit facilities made the city what it is. The bus, horse-car, electric trolley, and suburban train failed to keep pace with urban growth. Men had to live near their work. The city grew in the only direction open to it, toward the heavens. It assumed a perpendicular instead of a horizontal form. Inadequate transit intensified high land values. Bad means of transit and high land values made the slum. The city would have been a very different thing had transportation permitted it. It would have spread over a wide area.

Transit has begun to catch up with the city. It has opened up the country. In consequence the city is again being transformed: in this country by the suburban communities which encircle it; in Belgium by the sale of cheap workingmen's tickets on state-owned railroad lines which enable the workingman to travel twenty-four miles for two cents and live on the farms and in the far outlying villages.

In England improved transit has given birth to the garden suburb. It has made possible the Garden City. This is England's latest, possibly her greatest, contribution to the city problem, to the housing of the workingman, the clerk, and the moderately well-to-do classes of the great cities. The discovery came none too soon. For the city is sapping the vitality of Great Britain. In that country four people out of five live under urban conditions. And statesmen and reformers have stood aghast at the decay in the physical and moral fibre of the nation, due to the disease-breeding condition of the tenements and slums. London, Liverpool, Glasgow, Sheffield, all the large cities of Great Britain, have vainly

Frederic C. Howe, "The Garden Cities of England," *Scribner's Magazine*, **52**, No. 1 (July, 1912), 1-3.

struggled with the housing problem. They have built municipal dwellings, have tried to control private tenements, but the inrush of people swamped their most ambitious efforts.

The Garden City made its appearance about eight years ago. It marks the beginning of a change in the industrial, social, and domestic relations of society. It means that cities are to be rebuilt, that civilization is to change its forms, that the city of the future will be a far different thing from what it is today. It will occupy a very wide area. It will be beautiful, healthy, comfortable. It will urbanize the country. This in turn will ruralize the city.

The Garden City, too, is a shifting of emphasis from property to people, from the individual to the community. The motive which inspires it is the maximum of comfort, convenience, and happiness at the minimum of financial and personal cost. It marks a widening of community rights and an enlargement of community services. It means the building of the city by the city itself, from the foundations upward and from centre to circumference.

The Garden City idea has developed with great rapidity. It has not yet solved the city problem, nor has it stamped out the slum. It has shown how this can be done, however. And that is the first step to the solution of the problem. Birmingham is planning a suburb of 3,700 acres. Manchester has offered prizes for the best plans for developing a large outlying area and the building of cottages to rent from seven and one-half to ten dollars a month. Forty architects and landscape gardeners submitted plans to this competition. Suburban-building and garden-village projects are being carried out at Romford, a suburb of London, at York, Liverpool, Bristol, Hull, Rochdale, Ilford, Harborne, Ealing, Earlsworth, and elsewhere. These projects are being promoted by cities, cooperative companies, and private individuals. They have been made possible by the success of the Garden City and the enactment of a national town-planning law in 1909, which empowers local authorities to develop the territory surrounding a city as a comprehensive whole. The helplessness of the English cities, baffled for years by the tenement problem, by high disease and mortality rates and increasing poor taxes, has been changed to hope and enthusiasm. In a few years' time a score of public and semi-public garden developments have sprung up in various parts of the country. Most of these undertakings are tributary to a city. But all of them mark an abandonment of the barrack-like tenements and monotonous cottages of a few years ago and the substitution of beautifully planned suburbs, designed by landscape artists, out in the country where land is cheap and generous provision for health, recreation, and beauty is possible. For the housing of a people is a land as well as a transportation problem. A recognition of these economic foundations underlies all of the new housing projects.

The garden communities of Letchworth, Hampstead, Bournville, and Port Sunlight have demonstrated that clean, wholesome, comfortable cottages are possible for everybody and at the very low rent of from five dollars a month upward. They have demonstrated too that life is lengthened, the death and infant mortality rate is reduced, and labor is more efficient in these open-air communities than in the cities, and that working people gladly follow their employers to these more attractive surroundings.

In the building of garden villages three things are recognized as fundamental: one, the purchase of a large area of low-priced agricultural land in advance of any development; two, the permanent control of the whole area, as well as of streets, open spaces, and building regulations by the corporation or the city; and three, the reservation by the community, through the private corporation promoting the enterprise, of the increasing land values which the building of the community creates. The Garden City is in effect its own ground landlord. Indirectly it is a house-builder and house-owner. It operates through a private corporation which owns the land, pledged by its charter to limit its dividends to 5 per cent on the capital actually invested, and to use the speculative increase of land values for the community.

These are the physical foundations of the Garden City. To these are added, where necessary, the adjustment of transit to near-by cities so that rapid communication will be possible, as well as the ownership or a close working arrangement with the water, gas, and electricity supply. These form the plumbing of the city. They are essential to the life, comfort, and convenience of the people and the promotion of industry.

The main difference between the ordinary city and the Garden City is this: the former is left to the unrestrained license of speculators, builders, owners, to a constant conflict of public and private interests; the latter treats the community as a unit, with rights superior to those of any of its individual members. One is a city of unrelated, and for the most part uncontrolled, private property rights; the other is a community intelligently planned and harmoniously adjusted, with the emphasis always on the rights to the community rather than on the rights of the individual property owner.

There are three types of Garden Cities: (1), the self-contained industrial community like Letchworth; (2), the garden suburb, like Hampstead; and (3), the factory village built about a manufacturing plant by some large employer. Port Sunlight and Bournville are the best examples of the latter. All have the same underlying features of control by some superior community authority.

The idea originated with Mr. Ebenezer Howard, who published a book on Garden Cities in 1898 entitled *To-morrow*. From this dream the Garden City took form, and finally, in 1903, Letchworth was incorporated. It differs from the other Garden Cities in being an independent city with a complete municipal life of its own. It is an industrial city like Gary, Ind., with all the functions and activities of a self-contained community. And just as Gary was built by the United States Steel Corporation as a convenient place for the making of iron and steel products, just as it was planned in detail with reference to water and rail transportation, with provision for the needs of mills and furnaces, so Letchworth was planned as the home of all kinds of industries, with provision for the needs of workingmen, so that they would be healthy, and in consequence, efficient, so that well-to-do people would want to live there, so that manufacturers would find cheap building sites with cheap light, power, water, and fuel. Unlike Gary, Letchworth was planned for all its people, for the factory-worker as well as the factory-owner; for dividends in human health and happiness as well as on property.

part six

THE EMERGENCE
OF PROFESSIONAL
PLANNING

By 1909, City Beautiful ideals were beginning to recede in favor of the "City Efficient" or "City Scientific." This development was associated with the emergence of city planning as a profession and the establishment of permanent planning commissions within the structure of municipal government. Frederick Law Olmsted, Jr., son of the renowned landscape architect, outlined the early planner's perception of his role in the following address. He justified greater public control over land-use on the grounds that market disciplines had proven inefficient. They had not maximized health, wealth, and welfare. In Olmsted's view the city planner's responsibilities focused upon transportation and communication, public or quasi-public institutions, and the regulation of private property through zoning, building codes, and police power. The early professional planner concerned himself largely with the urban physical skeleton, and particularly with the circulation system.

Olmsted's definition of the planning function implied a greater public role in land-use decisions, but its significance for housing was limited and indirect. Housing is influenced by street arrangements, and these could be controlled to some degree by the planner. Six years after Olmsted's address New York City enacted the first comprehensive zoning law. Zoning became widespread during the 1920's and served as the chief practical link between planning and housing development.

New York's pioneer zoning measure was based upon the *Final Report* of the Commission on Building Districts and Restrictions. The selection from this document that is included here points to the curious alliance which swept zoning into hundreds of American communities. The potentialities of zoning impressed real estate interests and businessmen who wished to protect the value of their property. It appealed to planners and welfare experts who saw in bulk, height, and districting regulations an opportunity to control population density and to insure adequate light and ventilation in residential areas.

As far as housing was concerned, the defects of zoning soon became apparent. Like restrictive housing legislation, it provided municipalities with controls over physical development, and marked an important stage in the evolution of municipal planning. But like restrictive legislation, zoning was a negative tool. It did not clear slums, build houses, or provide a solid foundation for coordinated planning and housing policy. Equally important, it often served as an obstacle to creative, experimental subdivision planning.

Address on City Planning

Frederick Law Olmsted, Jr.

This subject of city planning, which we come hither to discuss in
some of its varied aspects, is no recent development. There is hardly
one of its principal phases that has not been represented as a practical
art ever since cities themselves began to be; and as a science, as a subject for theoretical discussion, it is probably but little less ancient. Yet
such a conference as this is a new sort of thing, and there is something
new about the subject today to account for such a conference. This new
thing is a growing appreciation of the close and vitally important inter-
relations between these varied lines of activity; of the profound influence which activities carried on in one part of the field and with
a view to one set of purposes may have upon the conditions in another
part of the field.

The complex unity, the appalling breadth and ramification, of real
city planning is being borne in upon us as never before, and one of the
main purposes of such a conference as this, I take it, is to assist workers
in all the different parts of this complex field to understand these inter-
relationships more clearly. The idea of city planning is one in which
all these activities—all the plannings that shape each one of the fragments that go to make up the physical city—shall be so harmonized as
to reduce the conflict of purposes and the waste of constructive effort
to a minimum, and thus secure for the people of the city conditions
adapted to their attaining the maximum of productive efficiency, of
health, and of enjoyment of life.

Frederick Law Olmsted, Jr., "Introductory Address on City Planning," Second National Conference on City Planning and the Problems of Congestion,
Rochester, New York, May 2-4, 1910 (Boston, 1910), pp. 15-30.

We are dealing here with the play of enormously complex forces which no one clearly understands and few pretend to; and our efforts to control them so often lead to unexpected and deplorable results that sober-minded people are often tempted to give up trying to exercise a large control, and to confine themselves to the day's obvious duty and let these remoter matters take their course.

And it is true that some sort of shifting equilibrium is sure to be reached in any case. Congestion, like most other evils, is self-limited. After congestion of population and the attendant ills reach a certain point (as they must have done in a good many mediaeval towns), the increasing death rate and the decreased attraction of town life owing to the misery offsetting its advantages must check any further increase, must produce an equilibrium.

Or take the simpler case of local congestion of street traffic: when with increasing congestion at any point the loss of time and other objections to passing through that point become so great as to neutralize the advantages to be gained by enduring them, the limit has been reached and additional people will cease to go there; other centers of concentration will tend to be developed, having relatively greater advantages and less tendency to become congested, and the congestion at the original center will tend to decline. Some 50 years ago one of the downtown street corners in New York became so congested and the congestion tended to so increase that it was felt to be quite intolerable. The city prepared plans for bridges, to carry foot passengers across the streets from sidewalk to sidewalk, and it was generally regarded as inevitable that some such grade separation should be made. But the congestion had become so great that teamsters and others found it more convenient to go elsewhere; business readjusted its habits; and presently the intolerable trouble was found to have cured itself.

To take an illustration from another field. There has been much concern for some years in Massachusetts over the tendency to rapid increase and congestion of population among the offspring of a certain class of very undesirable immigrants from Europe. Through an exercise of the police power, more ruthless than has been attempted even by the Indiana advocates of eugenics, the State has endeavored to put an arbitrary check upon the propagation of this undesirable class. The immigrants referred to, I ought to explain, are the European gypsy moths. In localities where they have been unchecked by man for a few years at a time they have so increased in numbers as to strip all the summer trees as bare as midwinter throughout large tracts of woodland, and by repeating such attacks have completely killed great numbers of trees. Where such congestion occurs the individual caterpillars making up the nauseous horde through lack of food become smaller and feebler and starve to death in great numbers. It is obvious that they could not advance to undespoiled territory on which to feed; they would in a year or two become extinct. If man and other enemies could keep out of the fight entirely, it is presumable that an equilibrium would be reached at about the point where there were just enough trees left alive in the country to feed the moths, and any further increase in the moths would so reduce the food supply as to check reproduction. In reality the other enemies of the moth make it probable that equilibrium will be reached somewhat short of that point, as it has been in Europe where the moth is a very troublesome pest but trees are still quite numerous.

To interfere with these complex natural forces, to attempt as we are doing to infect the moths with imported parasites of whose action we may be only half aware, is to get into very deep waters; it may involve a good many mistakes and may lead only to an unstable equilibrium, perhaps to one that is unexpected and undesired. An equilibrium of some sort is all that can be expected anyhow. Therefore, why not sit back and wait for the natural equilibrium of the matter, of their food and of their enemies, and then get used to it?

That is the comfortable, pious, stand-pat attitude; it saves a lot of mental effort and anxiety, it leaves more time for attending to the immediate duties and pleasures of life, and not seldom it leads to just as good results as to contest every step of the way with the half-understood forces that determine the outcome.

This is the old attitude in regard to the larger and more complex problems of what we now refer to as City Planning. But mankind will not be content with such an attitude after the imagination has grasped the larger possibility of control.

We cannot be content to let the free interplay of economic forces and social impulses pile up the evils contingent upon city life unchecked until a state of equilibrium is reached like that of the gypsy moths, in which the evils shall have become so great that the people can endure no more and continue to increase. Nor, when we fight these evils singly and begin to see here and there a part of the complex interwoven web of cause and effect that binds them all together with the things that make city life desirable, can we, as intelligent beings, fail to pluck at the web and try as best we may to untangle it, and begin to ask, each one of us in his own corner, "Will my cutting away of old threads and my building up of new hinder or help my brother who is working at some other tangle in his part of the field?"

But in addition to thus illuminating the connections which link the planning of all the diverse elements of the physical city together, and to thus giving each of us a more intelligent understanding of the purposes and principles controlling work in the less familiar parts of the field, such conferences as the present ought to open the way for substantial advances in each one of the subdivisions of the field, through better knowledge of facts, through clearer definition of purposes, and through improvements of technique.

It is plainly impossible at any one conference to deal with City Planning in any but a superficial or a fragmentary way; and as most of us have already obtained a good speaking acquaintance with the more important generalities that can be uttered on the subject, we come here mainly, I suppose, to exchange information about specific live questions with which we happen severally to have been brought into responsible contact. Yet in order that the larger relations may be kept in view, it has seemed best to include one general introductory paper, and I have been chosen as the instrument to rehearse what may be to many of you but familiar generalities.

City Planning may conveniently be considered under three main divisions.

The first concerns the means of circulation, the distribution and treatment of the spaces devoted to streets, railways, waterways, and all means of transportation and communication. The second concerns the distribution and treatment of the spaces devoted to all other public purposes. The third concerns the remaining or private lands and the character of developments thereon, insofar as it is practicable for the community to control or influence such development.

Facility of communication is the very basis for the existence of cities; improved methods of general transportation are at the root of the modern phenomenon of rapid city growth; and the success of a city is more dependent upon good means of circulation than upon any other physical factor under its control.

Moreover, the area devoted to streets in most cities (excluding those regions that are still undeveloped) amounts to between 25 and

40 per cent of the whole, and the improvement and use of all the remainder of the city area, both in public and in private hands, is so largely controlled by the network of subdividing and communicating streets, that the street plan has always been regarded as the foundation of all city planning. Indeed until recently in the minds of most public men in America general planning applied to cities has included nothing but the streets. But even as to streets, plans drawn primarily in the interest of easy communication, with a view to the common welfare of all the citizens, and by agents responsible for them, have been unusual.

It is an interesting consideration that most of the street planning in America, and until recently in Europe, has been done from the proprietary point of view. Nearly all new city and town sites that have been deliberately planned at all, have been planned by or for the proprietors of the site, largely with a view to successful immediate sales. Regard for the remoter interests of the community has commonly been dictated more by an optimistic opinion of the intelligence of prospective purchasers than by a disinterested desire to promote their future welfare. I do not mean to suggest that William Penn and his surveyors in laying out the original plan of Philadelphia consciously sacrificed the interests of its future inhabitants for the sake of their own convenience and profit in laying out and disposing of the property, or that Washington and Jefferson and Major L'Enfant and their associates in preparing the plans for the Federal City and putting the land thereof upon the market were consciously so influenced. I merely mean to call attention to the fact that the original layouts of practically all our cities and most of the "additions" thereto, except those which grew up without definite plans along lines developed to meet the temporary convenience of their inhabitants, have been drawn up by or for the original proprietor. Naturally where the proprietor or his agent has been enlightened and wise, even with a selfish enlightenment, the results have been relatively good for the community, and where he has been shortsighted and ignorant and mean in his selfishness the results have been bad; but the proprietary point of view must have colored and narrowed the outlook of the designers throughout. Moreover, the methods, traditions, and habits created in this school have inevitably dominated in large measure those official street planning agencies which the people of some cities have subsequently established with the purpose of exercising a control in the interest of the whole community over the street layouts of individual proprietors.

It is to be noted further that the ruts in which the planners of street plans have generally been running in America were deeply worn before the beginnings of modern revolution in means of transportation, dating from the introduction of metal rails and the development of the steam engine. Yet that revolution has been made by such moderate successive steps, and the men to whom the improved transportation is due have so seldom had any responsibility for street planning, and have so generally had their attention absorbed in the immediate practical problems, getting improved means of transportation as easily and cheaply as they could under the actual conditions which they found confronting them, that street planning has gone along in the same old routine way, and each improvement in the means of urban transportation has been fitted to the old procrustean bed of the street planner.

Steam railroads, it is true, developing as they did mostly in the open country, early began to learn the extent to which their efficiency depended upon a standard as to ease of curvature and lightness of gradient that put their planning in a wholly different category from that of the old type of thoroughfare; and somewhat more slowly they began to learn the importance of a complete separation from other kinds of traffic even at crossings. Although in the earlier days the existing streets were often used by the railroad in entering or passing through a town, as in the familiar cases along the New York Central, the tendency became gradually stronger to disregard the hampering streets and lay out steam railroads, even in cities, upon functional lines suitable to great long-distance thoroughfares operated at high speed. This divorce meant a great improvement as to the railroads, but it left the street system to stagnate in the old ruts, and tended to a total disregard of the relation between the streets and the railroads as distinct but complementary parts of one system of circulation.

But if the long-distance and suburban steam railroads thus divorced themselves from the antiquated methods of the street planners, all other improved means of transit have been as a rule bound hand and foot by them. Horse cars, mechanically propelled street cars of all sorts, and rapid transit railways, whether above or below the street grade, have generally been limited to streets laid out on plans that embodied scarcely any features that had not been common in city street plans for many centuries. The one important exception was that the average width of streets became greater. The routes which transit lines have had to follow have often been full of angular turns, have seldom been well distributed in relation to the area and the population, and in the case of surface lines have been encumbered by a large amount of general vehicular traffic for which adequate provision separate from the car tracks has been lacking.

It has thus been the tendency of street planners, whether acting for the city or for landowners, to give inadequate attention to the need of the public for various types of main thoroughfares laid out with sole regard to the problems of transportation, and to permit the supposed interests of landowners and fear of heavy damages to limit the width of thoroughfares and force them out of the best lines in order to conform to the owners' preferences as to land subdivision—usually conforming to a gridiron plan. But at the same time there has been, on the other hand, a decided tendency on the part of official street planners to insist with a quite needless and undesirable rigidity upon certain fixed standards of width and arrangement in regard to purely local streets, leading inevitably in many cases to the formation of blocks and lots of a size and shape ill adapted to the local uses to which they need to be put. The typical instance of the latter tendency is that of insisting on wide blocks and deep lots in a district occupied by people whose rents must be low and accommodations correspondingly limited; narrow, deep, dark buildings or rear tenements or both are the almost inevitable economic result. Another instance is that of fixing a minimum width of street and minimum requirements as to the cross section and construction thereof which makes the cost needlessly high for purely local streets, and thus inflicts a wholly needless and wasteful burden of annual cost upon the people.

Without more than alluding to the immensely important and complex relations between the railroad freight lines and terminals, the wharves, the waterways, the sites for economical warehousing and manufacturing, and the street system, I can say in summary that there is great need of treating all the means of circulation in a city as a single connected system, and at the same time of recognizing clearly the differentation of all its parts, so that each shall fit its function simply but without waste, from the biggest railroad terminal down to the smallest alley.

The second main division in city planning is a very miscellaneous one, including all the public properties in a city not used primarily for circulation; but they may be grouped for our purposes into three principal classes.

The first class may be called that of central institutions, serving the whole city and requiring for convenience a comparatively central position; such as the city hall and the head offices of public departments and services municipal and otherwise, the public library, museums, central educational establishments, and the like, together with the grounds appurtenant to them. Functionally it is important to class with these as far as practicable similar institutions of a quasi-public sort, even though owned and operated by private individuals or corporations, such as the leading establishments devoted to public recreation, dramatic, musical, and otherwise, with a clientele covering the whole city. One of the greatest needs in regard to all matters of this sort is the application of intelligent effort to the grouping of such institutions at accessible points in so-called civic centers for the sake of convenience and of increased dignity and beauty.

The second class consists of institutions serving limited areas and therefore needing to be repeated in many different places throughout the city. Such are schools, playgrounds, gymnasia and baths, branch libraries, branch post offices, police stations, fire-engine houses, district offices and yards of the department of public works and other public services, neighborhood parks and recreation grounds, voting places, public and quasi-public halls and social centers, and so on, including in the same class, so far as practicable, the local institutions conducted by private organizations, such as churches. The most notable thing about this class of institutions is that, while most of them belong to the city and are therefore entirely under the city's control as to location and character, the selection of sites is ordinarily determined by separate departments without the slightest regard to the selections of other departments or the possibilities of economy, convenience, and esthetic effect that might result from combination or grouping. Even in the separate departments it appears to be a rare exception that any considerable degree of comprehensive foresight is exercised in selecting sites with a view to economy of purchase or to securing a convenient and equitable distribution.

We shall not have intelligent city planning until the several departments responsible for the selection of sites for all the different public purposes of a local character get together in laying out a general plan and method of securing such sites, forming in many cases local civic centers in which the respective neighborhoods can take pride.

We must come, I believe, to a full acceptance of the principle, now well established in some of the German states, that when any tract of land in or adjoining a city is opened up for building purposes, not only the necessary streets must be set apart and dedicated to the public, but also all the other areas that will be required to meet properly and liberally, but without extravagance, all the public needs of that locality, when fully occupied, just so far as those needs can be foreseen by intelligent and experienced men. In no other way can the sites for these local institutions be placed so well or with so little economic waste.

The third class of public properties consists of many special institutions not demanding a central location but serving more than a local need, such as hospitals, charitable and penal institutions, reservoirs and their grounds, large parks and outlying reservations, parkways, cemeteries, public monuments, and certain monumental and decorative features to be found in connection with open spaces that exist primarily for other purposes. In this class the opportunities for economy and better effects through combination and grouping of sites are not so numerous, and what seems to be most needed is a more far-sighted regard for the relation of each of these important institutions to the probable future distribution of population and to the main transportation routes. In every case the adaptability of the site to its particular purpose needs to be considered with the best of expert advice, but in addition those which occupy considerable areas, like the large parks and cemeteries, need to be considered from a double point of view, as obstructions to the free development of the street and transit systems and as places to and from which large numbers of people must be carried by those systems.

The third main division of the lands within a city, consisting of all that remains in private ownership, is subject to public control chiefly in three ways.

The street plan absolutely fixes the size and shape of the blocks of land, and hence limits and largely controls the size and shape of individual lots and of the buildings which can be most profitably erected upon them.

The methods of taxation and assessment greatly influence the action of landowners, and of those having money to invest in land, buildings, or building mortgages. They have a direct influence upon the speculative holdings of unproductive property; upon the extent to which development is carried on in a scattered sporadic manner, involving relatively large expense to the community for streets, transportation, sewerage, etc., in proportion to the inhabitants served; upon the quality and durability of building; and, in those states where property is classified and taxed at varying rates, upon the class of improvements favored. Exemption from taxation for a certain period or other such bonus is a familiar device in some cities to encourage a desired class of developments, such as new factories.

But the chief means of planning and controlling developments on private property is through the exercise of the police power. The principle upon which are based all building codes, tenement house laws, and other such interferences with the exercise of free individual discretion on the part of landowners, is that no one may be permitted so to build or otherwise conduct himself upon his own property as to cause unreasonable danger or annoyance to other people. At what point danger or annoyance becomes unreasonable is a matter of gradually shifting public opinion interpreted by the courts.

The first object of building codes and of the system of building permits and inspections through which they are enforced is to ensure proper structural stability. A second object is to reduce the danger of fire to a reasonable point. A third object is to guard against conditions unreasonably dangerous to health. Tenement house laws, factory laws, and other special provisions operating in addition to the general building code of a city are directed mainly toward the protection of people using special kinds of buildings against unhealthful conditions and against personal risk from fire and accident. Buildings are classified according to the purposes for which they are used, according to their location with respect to arbitrary boundaries (such as "fire limits"), according to the materials of which they are built, and in dozens of other ways; and for each class minute and varied prescriptions and prohibitions are made which in the aggregate play an important controlling part in determining the size, height, purposes, plan, general appearance, and cost of building which the owner of any given lot can afford to erect within the law. While these regulations are intended only to guard against the evil results of ignorance and greed upon the part of landowners and builders, they also limit and control the operations of those who are neither ignorant nor greedy; and it is clear that the purpose in framing and enforcing them should be to leave open the maximum scope for individual enterprise, initiative, and ingenuity that is compatible with adequate protection of the public interests. Such regulations are and always will be in a state of flux and adjustment, on the one hand with a view to preventing newly discovered abuses, and on the other hand with a view to opening a wider opportunity of individual discretion at points where the law is found to be unwisely restrictive.

It is to be hoped that with increasing precision and scope of knowledge these regulations will become more and more stable. Especially in regard to structural stability it will certainly become possible, with improvements in the scientific basis for the regulations, to ensure the needful strength with a much smaller margin of wasted material and money than is now demanded to cover the vague doubt of the public authorities as to what the safe limit really is. So also in regard to the important detail of plumbing regulations, it seems likely that the future will bring a simplification and lessening of the present costly requirements rather than increased stringency. It is different with the regulations which have the most important effect upon the heights and widths and general plan of buildings, upon their relations to each other and to the streets, and thus upon the whole fabric of the city plan. These regulations are among the newer additions to the building laws; they are as yet tentative, unsystematic, half-hearted, and based upon no adequate recognition of the evils to be met. It is therefore likely that in this field there will be numerous changes for some time to come, and a tendency to much more radical requirements. The amount of light entering any given window in a city, and up to certain limits the amount of air, is dependent mainly upon the distance to the next opposite building wall and the height thereof above the level of the window. An examination of the building codes and tenement house laws of 35 American cities shows a confusing diversity in the regulations limiting building heights and horizontal spaces to be left open, and there are some cities in which there is practically no effective regulation at all.

A most profitable and fertile subject for study and discussion in this part of the field, to which some attention will be given at this conference, is that of the zone or district system of building regulations, under which the outcome of unrestrained economic competition in producing tall crowded buildings with badly lighted lower stories is recognized and accepted to a certain degree in the central parts of a city, but increasingly better standards of light and airiness are fixed in the outer regions where congestion has not yet progressed so far.

As to the influence of methods of taxation in determining the physical improvements undertaken on private property it will be enough here to cite a single example. In Pennsylvania the law provides for a classification of land as agricultural, rural, and urban, of which the second is taxed twice as much as the first in proportion to its value, and the third three times as much as the first. As applied within city boundaries, vacant fields held for speculative purposes are commonly taxed as agricultural property. Under these circumstances the man who draws his savings out of concealed and untaxed intangible investments and builds a house is not only punished by a tax on the money he puts into his house, but is taxed two or three times as much on the land as his speculative neighbor who does nothing but play dog in the manger and wait for "unearned increment."

The principle of classifying taxable property and discriminating in rates is closely akin to the protective tariff system, and is plainly open to the same sort of abuse of special privilege, as instanced by the above example from one of the strongholds of Protection and of special privilege, but it is undeniably a convenient and useful means of controlling in the public interest certain things which it is impossible or undesirable to reach through the police power. There is now pending an amendment to the Massachusetts Constitution to authorize the legislature to permit such discriminatory taxation. It is a very dangerous two-edged weapon. But so is nearly every weapon that is sharp enough to cut; the drafting and enforcement of building codes reek with graft where they are not under the intelligent scrutiny of an awakened public conscience; there is no means of advance that is guaranteed to be safe, painless, and untainted.

Bound up with the effect of taxation upon the physical constitution of cities, upon housing conditions and congestion, is the still more controversial subject of customs of land tenure; of the policy of long-term building leases with their great encouragement to new building on small capital as in Baltimore, and with their tendency to strangle any further improvements or changes as the term of the lease draws on; of the advantages and disadvantages and controlling conditions of the habit prevailing in many cities of home-ownership, and of the contrary habit elsewhere among people of the same standing of living in hired houses or tenements; of the relation of these habits to the desirable type of house and size of lot and of block in each city; of the co-partnership system of owning and leasing; of the position of the city as an active factor in the real estate market; of municipal tenements and municipal cottages; and so on. No thorough discussion of congestion or of city planning in the broad sense can long avoid such questions as these, and to take them up means touching some very live wires.

I have outlined in a fragmentary sort of a way the three main divisions of the city planning, dealing respectively with the lands devoted to the means of public circulation, the lands devoted to other public purposes, and the lands in private ownership. Within all of these divisions the actual work of city planning comprises the following steps: a study of conditions and tendencies, a definition of purposes, a planning of physical results suitable to these purposes, and finally the bringing of those plans to execution through suitable legal and administrative machinery. Every one of those steps of progression is vital, every part of the three main divisions of the field is important. At this conference several parts of the field will be touched upon, and they will be considered sometimes from the point of view of one step of progression, sometimes from another. I hope that these very general and superficial remarks of mine may help to make clearer the relationship between the apparently diverse matters that will be discussed.

In all that I have said you may have noticed the absence of any reference to beauty in city planning; that is because I want in closing to emphasize the relation which it bears to every phase of the subject from beginning to end.

The demands of beauty are in large measure identical with those of efficiency and economy, and differ merely in demanding a closer approach to practical perfection in the adaptation of means to ends than is required to meet the merely economic standard. So far as the demands of beauty can be distinguished from those of economy, the kind of beauty most to be sought in the planning of cities is that which results from seizing instinctively with a keen and sensitive appreciation the limitless opportunities which present themselves in the course of the most rigorously practical solution of any problem for a choice between decisions of substantially equal economic merit but of widely differing esthetic quality.

Regard for beauty must neither follow after reward for the practical ends to be obtained nor precede it, but must inseparably accompany it.

In his admirable and inspiring book *Town Planning in Practice* Raymond Unwin says:

> So long as art is regarded as a trimming, a species of crochet-work to be stitched in ever-increasing quantities to the garments

of life, it is vain to expect its true importance to be recognized. Civic art is too often understood to consist in filling our streets with marble fountains, dotting our squares with groups of statuary, twining our lamp posts with wriggling acanthus leaves or dolphins' tails, and our buildings with meaningless bunches of fruit and flowers tied up with impossible stone ribbons.

Report on Building Districts
and Restrictions

City of New York

Heretofore we have attacked the problems of public health and safety, as related to building development, in a piecemeal way. Special regulations have from time to time been provided with relation to tenement houses, factories, garages, theatres and other classes of buildings. Such regulations are often rendered wholly or partially ineffective by failure to control the environment of the building. The Tenement House Law provides for minimum size yards and outer courts which really depend for their adequacy on their being supplemented by similar yards and courts on adjoining lots. If, however, a towering loft building or warehouse is built next to a tenement, the standards of light and air aimed at in the Tenement House Law are impaired. The districting plan makes it possible to provide suitable and reasonable regulations for each class of buildings and at the same time preserves the advantage of substantially uniform regulations as to building height and yard depth for all structures within the block.

Every city becomes divided into more or less clearly defined districts of different occupation use, and type of building construction. We have the central office and financial district, loft districts, waterfront and industrial districts, retail business districts, apartment house and hotel districts, tenement house districts, private dwelling districts. Generally speaking, a building is appropriately located when it is in a section surrounded by buildings of similar type and use. Strong social

City of New York, Board of Estimate and Apportionment, Committee on the City Plan, *Final Report of the Commission on Building Districts and Restrictions,* June 2, 1916 (New York, 1916), pp. 12-14.

and economic forces work toward a natural segregation of buildings according to type and use. In general, the maximum land values and the maximum rentals are obtained where this segregation and uniformity are most complete. One purpose of districting regulations is to strengthen and supplement the natural trend toward segregation.

In spite of the natural trend toward segregation, building development in many parts of the city is haphazard. The natural trend toward segregation and uniformity is not strong enough to prevent the sporadic invasion of a district by harmful or inappropriate buildings or uses. Once a district has been thus invaded, rents and property values decline, loans are called, and it is difficult ever to reclaim the district to its more appropriate use. Individual property owners are helpless to prevent the depreciation of their property. The districting plan will do for the individual owners what they cannot do for themselves—set up uniform restrictions that will protect each against his neighbor and thus be of benefit to all.

While in New York City economic forces tend to the segregation of industries of the heavier type along the water and rail terminals, and to the segregation of certain light industries near the wholesale, retail, hotel and passenger terminal center in Manhattan, there are many kinds of light industry that are free from any segregating force and locate indiscriminately throughout the city. They are found scattered throughout the business and residential sections, especially the residential sections, from which their labor supply is recruited. The factory is usually a blight within a residential section. It destroys the comfort, quiet and convenience of home life. There is nothing more vital to the city than the housing of its people. The exclusion of trade and industries from the residential streets is essential to wholesome and comfortable housing. Stores, garages and other business buildings scattered among the residences are a constant menace to residence property. The concentration of all the neighborhood business buildings on the business streets makes the transaction of business more convenient. The segregation of dwellings on the exclusively residential streets adds to the convenience, quiet, and amenities of home life, and thus tends to increase property values on such streets.

In New York City the purely private injury incident to haphazard development has become so serious and widespread as to constitute a great public calamity. Through haphazard construction and invasion by inappropriate uses the capital values of large areas have been greatly impaired. This destruction of capital value, not only in the central commercial and industrial section of Manhattan, but also throughout the residential sections of the five boroughs, has reached huge proportions. It does not stop with the owners in the areas immediately affected, but is reflected in depressed values throughout the city. Market value for investment purposes is always affected by the hazard of the business. Economic depreciation due to unregulated construction and invasion by inappropriate uses has become a hazard that must be considered by every investor in real estate. This extra hazard increases the net earning basis required to induce investment, and consequently lessens capital values throughout the city. Whatever the capitalized amount that may be properly charged to the economic depreciation hazard, it is certainly a huge burden and one that affects not only the individual owners of real estate throughout the city but the savings and other large lending institutions, the municipal finances, and the general welfare and prosperity of the whole city.

There is an intimate and necessary relation between conservation of property values as here proposed and the conservation of public health, safety, and general welfare. Throughout a city the areas in which values have been depressed by the invasion of inappropriate uses or lack of building control as to height, courts, and open spaces, are the areas in which the worst conditions as to sanitation and safety prevail and where there is the greatest violation of the things essential to public comfort, convenience, and order. The decline in property value in such districts is merely an economic index of the disregard of essential standards of public health, safety and convenience in building development. Moreover, a depressed district of changing occupancy is almost always a district in which unwholesome home and work conditions prevail. The old building altered to suit a new use is usually very faulty in light, air, and sanitation. Declining values make it difficult or impossible to enforce proper standards. These depressed districts create the most difficult and perplexing problems in the establishment and administration of housing and factory regulations.

Moreover, the enormous losses sustained by owners of loft and tenement property will be a serious handicap to the provision of future buildings to house the increasing population and the rapidly expanding industrial development. This may become a very serious matter from the point of view of cheap and adequate housing and safe and convenient factory space.

With some eight billions already invested in New York City real estate and the certainty of added billions in the coming years, a plan of city building that will tend to conserve and protect property values becomes of vital importance not only to individual owners but to the community as a whole. Why not protect the areas as yet unspoiled and insure that the hundreds of millions that will be spent in the improvement of real estate in the coming years shall contribute to the solid and permanent upbuilding of this great city. Permanence and stability can be secured only by a far-sighted building plan that will harmonize the private interests of owners and the health, safety, and convenience of the public.

part seven

CONSTRUCTIVE
HOUSING
LEGISLATION

The handful of homes for workers built in Lowell in 1917 by the Massachusetts Homestead Commission might be described as America's first "public housing" project. In existence between 1911 and 1919, the MHC was unusual for its broad conception of the housing problem in an era which stressed restrictive legislation. The Commission's major goal was to reverse the population flow into cities. This necessitated a comprehensive housing program, which benefited from state financial assistance and careful attention to matters of design and site-planning. It also required a kind of regional planning which would rejuvenate country life. As the following selection suggests, the Commission was motivated by a belief that contact with nature was indispensable to a humane existence. The Commission thus emphasized the importance of garden plots attached to workers' homes.

World War I launched the first federally assisted public housing program in the United States. This experiment in public housing proved far more influential than the efforts of the MHC. Federal agencies built or supervised the construction of thousands of dwelling units for war workers and their families. Architects and planners were given an unprecedented opportunity to experiment with design, site-planning, and wholesale community development. The selection from the *Report* of the United States Housing Corporation indicates that the federal agencies aspired to create not houses alone, but total residential environments.

State Aid for Housing

Massachusetts Homestead Commission

THE RECOMMENDATION, AND SOME REASONS FOR IT

The Homestead Commission renews its recommendation of last year for an appropriation sufficient to allow an experiment or demonstration to be made in providing wholesome, low-cost homesteads, or "small houses and plots of ground," for "mechanics, factory employees, laborers and others in the suburbs of cities and towns," and accompanies the bill with detailed plans.

The principal considerations which induce the Commission to make this recommendation are:

1. There are not enough wholesome, low-cost dwellings.
2. There is no prospect that present methods will ever supply enough unless the State encourages their construction.
3. Therefore the State should experiment to learn whether it is possible to build wholesome dwellings within the means of low-paid workers.

Up to the time of the present great war every progressive country, without loss and generally without expense to the taxpayers, was doing something to promote the construction of dwellings for workers. Germany had built and financially aided in the building of many thousands of such dwellings. Since the war began England has enormously in-

Commonwealth of Massachusetts, *Fourth Annual Report of the Homestead Commission, 1916,* Public Document No. 103 (Boston, 1917), pp. 7-15.

creased her expenditures for this purpose. New Zealand's activities, the most extensive of any, show a profit to the public treasury of nearly half a million dollars per year.

History of the Bill. The original instructions given to this Commission were to draw a bill under which, "with the assistance of the Commonwealth, homesteads, or small houses and plots of ground, may be acquired by mechanics, factory employees, laborers, and others in the suburbs of cities and towns." Such a bill was submitted by the Homestead Commission to the General Court of 1912. Its principal provision was that the uncalled-for savings banks deposits in the State treasury might be used for the purpose proposed. The constitutionality of such use of these funds being questioned, queries were submitted to the Supreme Court on that point, which body in a sweeping and unanimous opinion declared that the use of any funds over which the State had control, for the purpose of aiding citizens to acquire homes, was contrary to the provisions of the Constitution.

Since that time a constitutional amendment permitting the taking of land for such a purpose was passed by overwhelming majorities in both branches of the Legislature in 1914 and 1915, and ratified by the voters by nearly a three to one majority in 1915. In consideration of this removal of the constitutional obstacles to legislation, the Homestead Commission in 1916 felt it to be its duty to revert to the instructions given to it by the Legislature in 1911, and to report to the General Court a new bill providing for a moderate, conservative, carefully conducted experiment, or demonstration, in order that experience might show what may properly be done, with safety to the Commonwealth and benefit to the public, to aid workers seeking to acquire homes. In support of this bill, which called for an appropriation of $50,000, the Homestead Commission presented to committees, somewhat in detail, information regarding the location and cost of certain pieces of land suitable and available for the purpose, and photographs, plans, specifications and cost of certain houses already built of the kind needed. Nevertheless, the passage of the bill was strongly opposed in both houses, the main contention urged against it being that no detailed plans accompanied the recommendation; and although it passed the lower House by a vote of 113 yeas and 86 nays, in the Senate it was defeated by a tie vote, 19 to 19. In renewing its recommendation of last year, therefore, the Commission deems it essential to submit with this year's bill carefully drawn plans for definite, concrete projects, in specified locations, giving as full details as is possible with the time and funds at its disposal.

Previous reports of the Commission have set forth with much detail the shortage and great need of good homes within the means of the low-paid workers of the Commonwealth; the wretched and repulsive conditions in which thousands of families live; the morally debasing and physically and mentally deteriorating tendency of such conditions; their injurious effects on the general public health and well-being; the facilities they offer for the spread of disease, particularly tuberculosis; the excessive loss of life among infants and young children; the undue amount of delinquency and moral and mental deficiency and lessened efficiency among dwellers in such houses; the lowered standard of citizenship which results from these causes; the constantly increasing tenement house population; the increasing flow of people from country to city and its ill effects in relatively decreasing the supply of food with increasing demand; the effects in congestion of population and unemployment of the constant influx from the rural districts with no corresponding flow of people away from the cities. The reports also describe the measures taken by other countries to alleviate these conditions, and the results of such activities, showing that Massachusetts and the United States are far behind all other progressive countries of the world in efforts to deal with this subject.

GENERAL STATEMENT REGARDING PLANS

In order to work out its plans the Commission desired to select one tract of land within reasonable walking distance of the industries of a manufacturing city, to be divided into plots to furnish room for (1) house and small garden, accommodating about eight families to the acre; (2) another tract within a 5-cent car ride, to be divided into plots varying from one-eighth to half an acre each; and (3) a third more distant tract to be divided into plots varying in size from one-half acre to five acres. It was found inadvisable to attempt to carry out the plans for the third project, largely because of lack of funds. The results of the Commission's work on the first two projects are presented herewith.

Minimum Requirements for Wholesome Homesteads

The Commission approves the statement that the ideal homestead is the single family house, preferably detached, with plot of ground. For such a home, what are the minimum requirements?

To answer this question it is necessary, first, to determine who most need such homes, how much they can pay, and what are the actual necessities for wholesome living.

Who Most Need Such Homes. There were 411,115 adult males employed in 1914 in the manufacturing industries of Massachusetts, 258,133, or 63 per cent, working for less than $15 per week. Of these, 98,330, or 24 per cent of the whole, received less than $10 per week. Probably a majority of these men are heads of families. Nearly all live in a few rooms in low-priced tenements, wholesome or unwholesome. Every consideration of public health, morals, well-being and progress and stability of civilization demands that the children of these men be brought up in wholesome, healthful homes. Yet almost the only dwellings available to them are the tenements, into which they are flocking in increasing proportions. The environment of the cheap tenement tends toward everything that is undesirable, but only a very few of the tens of thousands of families housed in such tenements can ever escape from them without aid. This is the class for whom provision should be made.

Amount They Can Pay. All authorities agree that the cost for rent should not exceed one-quarter the wages of the head of the household. Inasmuch as the income of the head of the families under consideration seldom exceeds $60 per month, the utmost they should pay is $15 per month for shelter. This appears to be too high for those receiving less than $15 per week, but it should be remembered that this Commission believes that there will be a considerable offset from the garden, for which provision should in every case be made. This is 9 per cent per year on a $2,000 homestead. A gross return of 9 per cent on such an investment appears to be as low as is safe, whether property is sold or rented. Can wholesome dwelling places be supplied within that figure?

Actual Necessities for Wholesome Living. Assuming an ordinary family—parents and children of both sexes—the house should have at least:

Living room, kitchen, 3 bedrooms, closets, cellar.
Cooking, heating, lighting, washing, toilet and bathing facilities.
Provision for drainage, sewage and garbage disposal.

There need not be a heating system, but provision should be made for stoves, other than cooking range, in places needed, and construction may well allow for a future heating system. The structure should be made as fire-resisting as possible with due consideration to cost.

The words of the act relating to homesteads preclude consideration of tenement houses, but there is one form of construction known as "semi-detached," more commonly hereabouts called a "double" house, which should receive some attention. In this case two houses are joined by a vertical party wall. Each house is complete in itself, and entirely separate from the other except for the party wall. Some examples of this method are to be seen in New England, but it seems not to have been greatly favored. It is freely used abroad, however, in the various better-housing enterprises. Its manifest advantage over the single house is economy in construction and in land. The principal objection to it is that it is a step away from the ideal single-family home toward the multiple dwelling. Where sufficient land is available the social advantages of houses entirely separate probably outweigh the economies effected by semi-detached construction. Some illustrations of semi-detached houses are included in the plans submitted.

Land enough for a garden, small or large, should go with each house. Sunlight and fresh air, plenty of both, are as essential to good health, happiness and general well-being as are food, clothing and shelter. To secure them there must be space—a "plot of ground"—around the home. Its proper and profitable use should be insisted upon. Competent instruction and supervision should be provided.

Some Benefits of Such Homes. We have thus summarized what seem to be the minimum requirements for such a homestead. The social and individual benefits to be derived are beyond calculation. They have been so fully considered in previous publications of this Commission that extended reference to them here is unnecessary. It may be well, however, briefly to restate some of them:

A saving of lives, particularly of children and infants
Better health, public and individual

Less opportunity for the contraction and spread of tuberculosis and other communicable diseases

Wholesome and healthful environment

Space for play

Infinite increase in the chances for joy in living, particularly for children

A tendency to inspire and elevate, physically, mentally, morally, rather than to depress, dishearten and deteriorate

Opportunities for an enjoyable and profitable employment that leads to the most fundamental of all vocations and gives rich returns for spare-time work both for parents and children.

The Possibility of Providing Such Homes

The question recurs: Can such homesteads be brought within the means of low-wage workers? The problem is to supply a homestead with these minimum requirements for $2,000.

Is Suitable Land Available? The first necessity is suitable land. Can it be secured at a price low enough to justify its use for such dwellings? Obviously not in the high-priced, central portions of cities. The homes must be located in the suburbs, either within or without the boundaries, as circumstances may determine. Most cities have large tracts of undeveloped land within their limits, enough for immediate use and to last for some time in the future. Cambridge, Chelsea, Lawrence, and Somerville are exceptions, being almost completely built over, but near Lawrence there is much spare land. Boston has over 7,000 acres of unoccupied territory, but much of it within a 5-cent fare radius is held at too high a price to permit of its being used in this way. In or near the rest of the cities there appears to be plenty of available land at not too high cost. Inquiry easily disclosed over 160 acres of land, in four tracts, now on the market, within or close to Lawrence, at $200, $1,306.80, and $1,197.90 per acre; about 445 acres in five tracts in or near New Bedford at prices ranging from $100 per acre to $450 per lot of about 5,000 square feet, $3,920.40 per acre; one tract of more than 500 acres within a 5-cent fare of Fall River at $20,000, about $40 per acre; at Lowell, 66 acres for $3,000, or $45.45 per acre, 55 acres for $26,000, or $472.72 per acre, 40 lots of 5,500 square feet each for 1 cent per foot ($435.60 per acre), 2,000,000 square feet, or 45.91 acres, at $653.40 per acre, 33 acres for $1,500, or $45.45 per acre, 212 acres for $10,000, or $47.17 per acre. These are tracts upon the market in the summer of 1916 for immediate sale. Some of them are in fair condition for immediate building, but others would require much labor to fit them for use. All are within or close to the 5-cent fare radius. They represent only a small proportion of the tracts available, and mention is made of them here only to show that in most localities land is abundant at moderate prices.

This indicates that suitable suburban land can be acquired in or near to many cities at a cost ranging from $40 up to about $700 per acre. Subdivided into eight lots (nearly 5,000 feet per lot), there results a cost of from $5 to about $90 per lot. The expense for survey, bounds, preparation of soil, sewerage, water supply, roadways, curbs, walks, trees, etc., would be about $175 per lot in the urban development. In more distant developments the cost would be much lower, as a less expensive type of improvement would be appropriate, probably $80 or less.

For a development within city limits, then, there remains a balance not to exceed $1,735 for the construction cost of the house itself.

Perhaps as good a way as any to show what can be done for that sum is to give a few illustrations of what actually has been done in recent years in this country at about that figure. Various groups in different places have experimented on the problem of supplying wholesome houses for the poor at prices within their means. Some of the results of their work are herewith offered for consideration. No great amount of material is available for comparison, as most enterprises of this kind by employers or others have produced tenements, houses in rows, or houses either far above or far below the requirements and cost of $2,000, deemed by this Commission most nearly to meet the present needs in Massachusetts. Abundant material from other countries could be introduced, but conditions, methods of building, requirements and customs abroad differ so greatly from ours that details of construction appear to have but little value here. The lowest cost for government-aided cottages with plot of ground in Ireland is given as $750. In eastern European countries before the war the cost for such dwellings ran lower. In New Zealand the construction cost of State-aided dwellings was fixed at £300, which amount was gradually increased until in 1914 the total value of a State-aided worker's dwelling and lot must not exceed £750. "Workers' dwellings are now being erected on rural allotments of about five acres, with the maximum unimproved value of land of £250; this allows £500 ($2,500) for the cost of any building erected." In Queensland, Australia, it reaches a maximum of rather more than $4,800.

In presenting these illustrations of actual recent construction the Homestead Commission is not unmindful of rapidly increasing prices. It would be unwise and probably untrue to say that a house which cost a certain sum in 1915 or 1916 can be built for the same or approximately the same amount in 1917. Yet it is to be remembered that the higher prices go, the greater is the need of the poor. Nor can any important decrease in prices be expected in the near future. It would seem to be urgent, therefore, to proceed with an experiment at once, in order to meet the present need. Should declining prices later result in lower costs to build, a broader and safer work will be made possible by the experience gained under high prices.

Throughout this report wood construction has been considered almost exclusively, largely because that is the prevailing type in this locality. The Commission is aware that brick or other forms of durable construction may in the long run be more economical, and some study has been made of such methods as the various forms of concrete, hollow tile and stucco. We believe that several materials should be represented in this experiment, and that careful note should be made of results, so that future years might determine which is the most suitable and economical.

Federal World War I Housing

United States Housing Corporation

GOOD APPEARANCE A FINANCIAL ASSET

The Housing Corporation was well aware that good appearance would be a financial asset in the housing developments; that is, we knew that up to a certain point every householder would be willing to pay something extra for good-looking surroundings. But we realized also that in communities of people of modest means, such communities as the Housing Corporation was dealing with, the householders simply cannot afford very much expense, over and above what they must pay for the absolute necessities of life, purely for enjoyment of the appearance of their home neighborhood, however much they might desire this enjoyment.

This fact makes it very difficult for any small development of houses scattered among those of an existing large community to do much without financial loss to raise itself above the mediocrity or ugliness which too often surrounds it. But in a large development or an isolated development the case is entirely different. Here all the attractiveness of harmonious buildings pleasantly related, of street systems which have a general unity and a sensible fitness to the ground surface, of avoidance of the mutual nuisances which arise when buildings, often for different uses, are jumbled together in inconvenient relations—all this can often be had for no extra expense at all over the

United States Department of Labor, Bureau of Industrial Housing and Transportation, *Report of the United States Housing Corporation*, Vol. II: *Houses, Site-Planning, Utilities* (Washington, D.C.: Government Printing Office, 1919), pp. 71-74.

cost of houses and streets built without consideration of these relations.

If it is thus possible to get a community which has an air of well-being of its own, it is much more likely that the householders will make effort enough to maintain and better its appearance, each in his small way on his own lot. And of course the general pride of the householders in the attractiveness of the neighborhood is the force by which, in the long run, the appearance of the community will largely be determined.

In this chapter we have set down some of the ways in which we have found that it was possible to obtain some degree of order and attractiveness of appearance without incurring thereby an expense which the kind of people whom we were serving could not afford.

Ways of Obtaining Consistency

It will evidently go a long way to help the appearance of a town if as anyone goes along the streets he feels that each new view that he gets, each new neighborhood that he goes through, has some consistent character of its own.

The simplest way to make a street present a consistent "picture" is to have it form a vista. Anyone's natural tendency when in a straight street is to look down it. There should be something at the end to look at not too far away. In this respect the regular gridiron plan of streets of indefinite extent fails to be satisfactory. Every street in the gridiron is a vista, but no vista has any terminus. In many cases we planned streets with slight angles, or curved, or (in the case of purely local streets) ending abruptly against a transverse street; and arranged the buildings and plantings so that there should be pleasant views along the streets, both toward and from the buildings at the vista ends.

A section of street may be made distinctive by setting the houses close to the street at each end of the section and farther back in the middle, so forming or suggesting an inclosed space into which the houses look and each side of which is a consistently designed group or continuous row of houses. Sometimes where there was land enough we carried this idea so far as to make a neighborhood park or a village green with two roadways and a central grass space. The arrangement proved worthwhile, however, in many cases where the roadway was continuous and the difference in setback of the houses was less than ten feet.

An examination of the executed work, however, shows that in designing such variation in setback the tendency has been almost invariably to overdo the amount of the setback. The effect can often be quite adequately secured by a variation in setback of no more than two to six feet. Generally speaking, where front porches are used, a variation in setback of less than the width of the porch is more agreeable in every respect than where the porches of the recessed houses fall wholly behind the wall line of the more advanced houses. The amount of recessing which has proved desirable as a matter of appearance depends of course upon the length of the recessed portion; the shorter it is the less can it be recessed, the controlling principle being that the building fronts of the recessed portion should not entirely disappear from sight in the raking views along the street which are ordinarily those of most importance. In these views all projections and recessions from the normal building line count for their full dimensions in depth, whereas their lengths are extremely foreshortened.

A strong effect of consistency of design can be got by balancing a building or a group of buildings on one side of the street by a similar building or group on the other side. In monumental designs where two public buildings can reasonably be made alike there are, of course, many good examples of this. In dealing with small dwelling houses, on the other hand, we felt that a rigid similarity in a balanced composition is apt to spoil the individuality and homelikeness of the private dwellings, and to make the whole street look stiff, set, and institutional.

We found that on the whole in the work that we were doing it was better not to strain after obviously designed effect on every street, but to choose here a retired street for a quiet open space, there a street intersection for a more monumental treatment, and to have a large proportion of more ordinary streets leading up to the points of interest. At Briarfield, if the scheme were carried out according to the tentative house location plans as shown, the avenue from the store center to the school, having so much of interest at either end, would probably be better if along its length the houses were more similar and less interesting.

Street intersections are natural places for the designer to put some particular feature of interest, and this was the easier for us to do because we could economically put a larger building on a corner, where it got more light. We found on study, however, that when we were using single or semi-detached houses the only effect that could be got was a pleasant grouping of four buildings about the intersection, and not an inclosure of the intersection like a court. The buildings were too small and the streets too wide to make the latter possible. When we did endeavor to get the effect of a space inclosed on all sides or at one end, we used stores or row houses to make the larger architectural masses needed, and so arranged them around an open area that there was sufficient inclosing housefront proportionally to the openings made by the entering streets.

Where the people to be housed needed public or semi-public buildings like stores, schools, a moving-picture theater, or a community building, and the structures were grouped at an important road intersection, as a matter of appearance this was a very good thing. It gave a definite center and dominant point to the whole design, and the buildings, being larger and all serving a public purpose, could be more reasonably arranged for their general effect, perhaps inclosing a "square," as just suggested, or perhaps in a more open group.

Variety

When a project was large enough, and different districts in it were designed for different purposes, this, if rightly done from the point of view of use, gave also naturally a consistency of appearance in each district and variety in the whole project. Even when no particular districting was needed, and no difference in the ground made a variety of appearance, something of the same effect was possible by marking the difference between the larger thoroughfares and the quiet local streets, and giving one street, for instance, elms for street trees, wide planting strips and front-line hedges, and giving another street sugar maple street trees, with narrower planting strips and open front lawns.

The choice of the color of paint for the houses, the choice of stucco or brick or wood as a material, and the choice of material and color of the roofs, we attempted to use as a means of making various neighborhoods different, and each one consistent. We attempted to use differences of color in a subordinate way to multiply the variation due to differences in form between the houses of a given group. We were convinced that an attempt to get variety by using different colors of paint on houses which were all alike in form was likely to look forced, and that it was better to accept the similarity of house form as making the whole neighborhood consistent in appearance. We could still relieve the houses by different minor details of color of trim or form of porch or roof, and especially by planting of different vines to grow on the houses and different trees and shrubs, and by the use or omission of hedges or fences, and informal shrubbery along the front boundaries. It was probably in respect to color and texture of roofs that the limitations on material imposed by war conditions most conspicuously and unfavorably affected the appearance of our projects, as notably in the case of Cradock.

Much variety can be and was obtained with little or no expense by repeating the same house plan, but placing it with its side or with its end to the street, by reversing it right for left, by ringing a series of changes on the location of porches, and finally by using more than one shape of roof.

A consideration of all the projects, when they were sufficiently near completion to indicate their final appearance, made it very clear that an unpleasant monotony among the houses of a large project can be avoided by the skillful use of architectural variations surprisingly few in number and surprisingly limited in their range of architectural character (as, for example, at Watertown and at Aberdeen); and that any effort at a greater variety in the houses than can easily be obtained by such simple methods is apt to result in one of three unfortunate ways. The least unfortunate is a mere waste of effort and expense in producing a needless number of different plans all of an excellent sort, when two or three, with a few interchangeable variations, would accomplish the purposes. The second is the admission of confessedly inferior designs, of otherwise harmonious and acceptable sort, under the mistaken impression that the number of type designs must be increased. The third is the mingling of designs so different as to appear restless and forced, or even so different as to appear clashing and inharmonious. The introduction of such striking differences between the houses of any group or neighborhood, especially if the same striking difference is repeated several times, does not overcome the most serious aspect of monotony in a housing development, namely, the suggestion of institutionalism. It rather emphasizes the repetitive character of the work by appearing too loudly to deny it; whereas if the differences are not very striking, if there is no noticeable effort at differentiation, the fact that the modest and pleasant variations often repeat is not conspicuous.

Taking Advantage of Natural Features

When there was any existing natural beauty, either on our own land or visible from it, of course we did what we could to preserve it and display it to the best advantage.

We endeavored to preserve as parks and public spaces of various kinds, where these were needed, the most attractive bits of landscape that we found. Fortunately, the roughest land, and that with brooks and large trees, is likely to be both the most interesting to look at and walk through, and the most expensive to build on, and so on both counts best fitted for public reservations. We also studied carefully the distant views from our property, and where possible arranged that the best of them should be enjoyed not only from house windows but from some public resting place.

Similarly, if there was some ugly object near our development, we endeavored to screen it with planting, or turned the back of the layout upon it, if this was practicable.

Smaller natural features also we preserved where we could reasonably do so, even diverting a road to save a picturesque group of trees. This can be carried too far, however, for if a road is permanently made crooked to save a tree, when the tree dies—as it will, and probably all the sooner for the presence of the development—the crook in the road appears unreasonable.

It is especially difficult, where the houses have to be close together, to save many existing trees or other natural features, and for this reason we chose open and rolling areas for our housing sites where possible, in preference to more beautiful broken or wooded areas, for we knew that the greater natural beauty would prove only an added construction expense and be lost in the end when the project was completed.

Importance of General Effect of Buildings

Our experience has led us to recognize two errors, which are especially to be avoided by the designer in planning the appearance of a community—important errors, which may spoil the sale of the development. First, in seeking a unified effect the designer should not make all the houses and lots so much parts of one set and formal design that they look like a penal or charitable institution. Second, in seeking interest and picturesqueness he should not make all the houses so different, and each so unusual, with so much done evidently for effect that the whole looks like a village on the stage. Neither kind of development would find a ready market, and the reason in both cases would be at bottom the same; that people in this country want to live in independent, self-sufficient homes of their own in a real, complete American town, which they understand and run in their own way, and they do not want their houses to be, or to look like, parts of an artistic or sociologic experiment.

This is an example of the money value of what is indefinitely called the "tone" or "character" of a development, that is, the total effect made on the observer by its appearance. We were aware that it is possible to produce an unattractive character by overemphasized design, but we were convinced also that the character of our developments would be still more unattractive without the consistency of appearance due to simple and reasonable design. This belief had some influence in our avoidance of certain sites in a few localities where, because of existing structures, no consistency of design was possible in the new development.

The houses which can now be built for people of modest means are smaller than in the past, and in the less expensive suburban communities they have to be set close together to economize land and utilities. The relation of one house to another in appearance is therefore especially important in this kind of development, and there is an evident advantage from the point of view of appearance, in planning a development not scattered among existing houses but all in one piece, so as not to have small houses dwarfed by large ones, simple houses overpowered by ornate ones, or decent houses spoiled by shabby ones, and the whole spirit of the new work frittered away and lost by being mixed with buildings of another kind.

part eight

COMMUNITY PLANNING:
THE REGIONAL
PLANNING ASSOCIATION
OF AMERICA

The Committee on Community Planning of the American Institute of Architects (CCP) was formed in 1919. Several of its members, including Clarence Stein and Henry Wright, were later associated with the Regional Planning Association of America (RPAA). The two groups were linked by ideology as well as personnel. They differed, essentially, in the greater emphasis of the RPAA upon regional reconstruction. The document that follows combines the 1924 and 1925 *Reports* of the CCP. Prepared by Lewis Mumford from materials supplied by the Committee, it represents the views of the RPAA as well as the CCP.

The *Report,* which includes a sweeping historical indictment of traditional speculative development, delineates new architectural, housing, and planning policy. It emphasizes the advantages of large-scale group and community planning in lieu of the small-scale, speculative process of city-building. Particularly interesting is the interpretation of the architect's social responsibilities and the degree to which the existing legal and physical framework of the city inhibits his creativity. As a whole, the document attempts to clarify the relationship between physical and social planning, and provides, in this connection, a classic formulation of the architect's social role.

The Architect and the City

American Institute of Architects

PART I

I

Why has the American architect so little interest in city planning?
Twenty years ago, with the impetus derived from the Chicago Exposition and the resumption of L'Enfant's plan for Washington, he seemed
ready to take the leadership in the city planning movement. Today he
has abandoned it. How has this come about?

On the face of it, his indifference and his lack of initiative are
surprising. The architect's work in planning the individual house or
factory or office or public building is governed by the plan of the city;
the layout of the roads, the location of traffic thoroughfares, the size
and shape of lots, the innumerable legal restrictions that relate to
height, air space, and mode of construction; all these factors touch the

The American Institute of Architects, *Report of the Committee on Community Planning (to the Fifty-Eighth Annual Convention, 1925)*, reprinted
in pamphlet form.
    Note: The report of the Committee on Community Planning consists
of two parts: the first is the report of the committee of last year which was
approved by the Convention of the Institute in 1924. The second is a further development of the thought expressed in that report. These two, which
form a unit, are the result of the studies carried on over a number of years
during which time the personnel of the committee has but slightly changed.
. . . Some of the material has appeared in other form in the Journal of the
A.I.A. and the committee wishes to acknowledge its debt to the Editor, Mr.
Charles Harris Whitaker, for his aid and encouragement. It wishes furthermore to express its appreciation of the great help it has received from Mr.
Lewis Mumford in giving literary form to its studies.

architect's proper job and help or hinder it. Over these factors, however, he continues to exercise little or no control. While in most foreign countries the architects are the principal city planners, in America others first created the mangled regularity of the gridiron, and still control the form of our cities' growth.

The situation is all the more curious for the reason that the architect's training as an imaginative and at the same time practical planner obviously fits him for leadership in this work. For lack of his guidance as a community planner, some of the most admirable achievements in American architecture have been rapidly buried under the debris that marks the unending transformation of the American city. Aside from the architect's potential opportunity for service to the community in preparing the mould that will govern its future growth and activities, one would, perhaps, think he would insist upon taking the leadership, if only for his own protection. On the contrary, the city planning movement has fallen into the hands of specialists who are chiefly interested in isolated phases of city development. The transit expert, the municipal engineer, the real estate broker, the sanitarian combine to exert a far greater pressure upon the architect than his individual client; for both architect and client must work within the rigid frame that these special interests have, at one time or another, provided.

It is all but hopeless for the architect to design sanely and beautifully unless he can relate his individual works to a sanely and beautifully designed city, to a sane and beautiful community. If each particular work of the architect is to do its part, as the pieces in an orchestra perform their parts, it seems necessary that the architect himself should preside over the whole performance and take the place now occupied by the specialist who is concerned only with the wind or the strings or the brass, or the arrangement of the orchestra's chairs. The architect's actual task of bringing together all the arts necessary for the better ordering of cities and buildings has scarcely begun.

II

The Committee on Community Planning has felt that its most important function is to offer some constructive suggestions that might lead members of the profession to a more active participation in community planning. The committee, however, is faced at the beginning with the difficulty of drawing a line between what might be called superficially constructive suggestions and fundamentally constructive ones. It has finally come to the conclusion that the most positive action that can be taken at this time is a simple statement of the general problems of community planning, as it involves the work, the cooperation, and the position of the architect.

Our first effort is, briefly, to state the problem that confronts every community when it begins to think seriously of community planning. Here two choices are open. The first is the development of plans and suggestions which the uninstructed laymen would consider concrete, constructive, and practical. Under this head come such obvious matters as the widening of a traffic street, the placement of a new municipal building, or the provision of a playground. None of these matters carries with it the necessity of departing from the powers and precedents that almost every American community possesses. Every automobile driver knows when a street is congested; every mother knows when her child needs a place to play in; and the immediate remedy for each of these conditions is obvious. Things of this nature, some highly important and some trivial, belong to the routine of city planning practice.

There is a second kind of planning, however, which, while it works with the same materials and confronts the same problems as the first, does not arrive so easily at a solution. Confronted by a congested traffic avenue, it examines the alternatives between widening the roadway or creating, let us say, a new centre of business which will divert the stream of vehicles. Confronted by the necessity for a playground adjacent to a crowded district, it inquires whether the cost of buying out the existing property-rights in the necessary lots, together with the creation of a shortage of houses in this area, would be effectually compensated for by the provision of a recreation space, or whether the same purpose might not be served, as in recent London examples, by the creation of an independent garden suburb which would be designed from the beginning with sufficient play-areas.

This second type of planning may at times result in proposals which would involve a radical departure from the present adjustment of the community; such a departure as that under which the London County Council provides houses at cost, and in case of necessity below the current economic rent, to slum-dwellers whose habitations have been torn down. For the sake of clearness, we shall call the first type of planning, which is concerned chiefly with the physical properties of the city, "city planning." The second type, which considers the physical changes in due relation to the social situation of which they are a part, we shall call "community planning."

In order to account for the present position of the architect in the city planning movement, and in order to give the architect a more definite orientation towards his tasks and opportunities, we have found it necessary to review the history of city planning and the development of the American city itself. If the chief result of this survey seems mainly to center upon difficulties, upon bad precedents, upon lapses, it is only to pave the way for a more adequate conception of the tasks of community planning. This conception will avoid all that has proved inhumane and wasteful; and it will endeavor to point out the terms upon which the architect will be able to provide a more and more adequate shell for a more and more vitalized community.

III

Our present practices in land subdivision and street layout go back to the middle of the eighteenth century. Up to that time all the cities of the Atlantic seaboard, with the exception of Philadelphia, had been planned in piecemeal, with respect to their original functions as farm villages or port-villages; their irregular layout was based upon a direct consideration of the use to which the land would be put. In Cambridge, Mass., this method led perhaps at times to a too frequent subdivision of blocks, in order to get corner frontages; but at the same time it was flexible enough to provide those deep blocks with closed avenues leading to an interior plot which give parts of Cambridge and Longwood the unique charm that they still possess as residential districts.

By the middle of the eighteenth century the arbitrary rectangular block, planned in advance of use and without reference to use, had been incorporated with the plan of New York; a similar layout was adopted for Pittsburgh in 1795; and it was on this scheme of streets that L'Enfant superimposed his plan for Washington. Thomas Jefferson and others found justification for the formal rectangular layout in antiquity; its real justification, however, lay in the conditions that were then creating the commercial town. Those conditions were firmly in the minds of New York's city planning commissioners when in 1811 they blocked out the development of the city for the next century; and they remained in the minds of all their disciples and successors.

What were these conditions? The principal one, perhaps, was the dominance of traffic and trade. It was this that made the provision for traffic streets the chief task of New York's Commissioners, and since, without paying any attention to topographic difficulties or to the natural routes of travel they assumed that the maximum traffic would be across town, they placed their rectangular parcels lengthwise from river to river. One might write this defect down as a bad guess were it not for the fact that it so obviously ignored more fundamental needs in paying attention to the interests of commerce. Thus, it ignored the fact that in New York the houses under this street system would never receive direct sunlight on one side; whereas had the blocks run north and south all the houses would have had a double exposure. We bring out this particular point in order to emphasize the narrow basis upon which the commercial city was originally planned. Its chief, in fact its only interest, was the development of the apparatus for selling goods and land. In the gridiron scheme, as the commissioners naively confessed when they failed to provide for more open spaces, recreation and housing could take their chances; indeed, the amount of park space was deliberately reduced to a minimum in order not to put land out of the market.

Here we come to the second animus in the gridiron scheme, namely, the parcelling out of lots. In New York, the deep, narrow, rectangular lot was deliberately adopted because it "wasted" less land than irregular plots; it was for this reason, too, that diagonals and ovals, such as during the eighteenth century had given to Bath its charm and dignity, were set aside as frivolous. With plots of this description, land could be sold by the front foot; sales and transferences could be made without using a different legal formula; and lots could be marked out long before anyone knew whether a house, a shop, or a factory would eventually be erected on them. Both in street layout and land subdivision no attention was paid to the final use to which the land would be put; whereas the most meticulous efforts were made to safeguard its immediate use, namely, land speculation, and in order to further this use hills were graded, swamps and ponds filled, and streets laid out long before these expenditures could be borne by the people who, in the end, were destined to profit from or suffer by them. It was no wonder that the newer towns like Cincinnati, St. Louis, and Chicago by the middle of the nineteenth century had forfeited, to pay the cost of street improvements, generous tracts of land which the original planners had set aside for use as civic centers.

So successful was this type of planning from the commercial standpoint that it became the inevitable mould into which every American city was poured. The swiftness with which the rectangular plan could be laid out by the least imaginative of surveyors, the equal ease with which each block could be subdivided, lent itself to the haste of the pioneer. Once the original tract of the city was bounded, a day's work at the drafting board was enough to complete the plan itself. Even today this type of plan is repeatedly justified, by those who should know better, because of its convenience to the municipal engineer's offices.

The gridiron plan had one other defect which was accounted a virtue by the pioneer, and still is shared by those who have not profited by the intervening century's experience. With its avenues that continued into swamps and wildernesses, with its future growth forecast for at least a hundred years, it gave forth a promise of manifest destiny and captivated the imagination. Scarcely any American town during the nineteenth century was so mean that it did not aspire to grow faster than its neighbor, faster maybe than New York, and become a metropolis. Only by the assimilation of more and more people could its colossal city plan and its inflated land values be justified. If the older cities of the seaboard were limited in their attempts to become metropolises by the fact that their downtown sections were originally designed for villages, the villages of the middle west labored under just the opposite handicap; they had acquired the framework of a metropolis before they had passed out of the physical state of a village. The gridiron plan was a sort of hand-me-down which the juvenile city was supposed to grow into and fill. That a city had any other purpose than to attract trade, to increase land values, and to grow is something that, if it uneasily entered the mind of an occasional Whitman, never exercised any hold upon the minds of the majority of citizens. For them, the place where the great city stands *is* the place of stretched wharves, and markets, and ships bringing goods from the ends of the earth; that, and nothing else.

In this standardized street, block, and lot system, architecture and the other humane arts were simply left out of account. The rules of land subdivision in a community which expects to grow, which believes with an almost religious faith in the duty of growing, have to be made sufficiently broad to cover all sorts of possibilities. As a result, street widths, lot depths, and regulations as to setbacks have frequently been wasteful out of all proportion to the small single family houses which first occupied them; and at the same time they have proved quite as inadequate to serve the large tenements, business buildings, or lofts which came in at a later date. The pioneer's type of plan, by being ready for any emergency, actually meets none.

The effect of the monotonous gridiron system upon architecture has frequently been noted. The sameness of the plots, the absence of special sites, the sidelong approach to every building, great or small, inconspicuous or monumental, all tend to stifle the imagination of the architect and to do away with even such small variations or setbacks as might relieve the monotony of the continuous rows of houses that are so characteristic of our American cities. It is in its effect upon residential planning, however, that the American block and lot have exerted a positively baneful effect. As a result, we have dark interior rooms, wasteful corridors, and a tendency to build over areas that should be used for courts and gardens. The railroad and dumbbell tenements in New York, the equally badly lighted flats of St. Louis and other western cities, as well as the depressing row houses of Philadelphia, were planned to fit the requirements of lots rather than to serve the uses of the tenants. Even in some of the most fashionable apartment houses and hotels that New York can boast of, a large proportion of the rooms have either insufficient light or breadth of aspect. The overcrowding encouraged by our traditional lot plans is nothing but a dead loss. Financially, it means that the people who live in dark and poorly lighted quarters pay ample for what they get, while those who enjoy light and air pay something of a premium for it.

In fact, the outstanding evils of bad housing, inadequate light and ventilation, and the lack of privacy, are perhaps as often caused by narrow lot subdivision as by the overcrowding of the population. During the past few years, in the cheaper land areas around New York, there has been a tendency to develop small single and two-family houses instead of apartments. As a result we have 15 to 20 families per acre instead of the 100 to 150 in the former tenement districts. Nevertheless, in the greater part of this low-density housing the same narrow courts, inadequate lights, and the failure to observe privacy exist as in the high-density districts.

Again: there has been a striking demonstration during the last few years that apartments could be designed more economically if they covered a much smaller percentage of the land, provided that the old, narrow lot divisions were obliterated. Such apartment houses not only provide better light and ventilation, they even give a better return on the investment. In the same way, a plotting based on the proposed use of the land for small single-family and two-family houses, instead of on the convenience for selling and speculating, would not merely give the architect an opportunity to plan internal recreation areas; it would also enable him to effect a grouping of buildings, and to introduce simple elements of landscape design, features which today are eliminated from house-planning in cities and relegated to the country estates of the wealthy, almost the last refuge of architects in our communities. Here are two cases in which the architect's ability and invention have so far been able to contribute nothing to the enhancement of life in our cities, because of the fact that he so far has exercised no influence on community planning; and it is only in terms of community planning that these improvements can be introduced.

We must emphasize that the Standard American City plan has no place for these improvements. There is a complete lack of coordination between street and plot layout on one hand and the planning and grouping of houses and other buildings. All the architect's ingenuity and imagination are wasted so long as the frame within which he is forced to work is designed by others who have no concern for the kind of houses that people must live in, and who put the convenience of the drafting board or the legal document above the needs and desire of the community. The principal exceptions to this generalization about our cities are a few old New England villages, a handful of modern suburbs, and a number of small industrial villages, chiefly those that were built by the Shipping Board and the Housing Corporation during the war. Here, and here alone, if we exclude the estates of the wealthy, has the architect had an opportunity to put in practice the sort of comprehensive design which draws upon all of his resources, and takes the full measure of his professional equipment.

It comes to this: it is almost impossible to demand that the architect deal honestly and thoroughly with the part when he has no control over the whole. The architect's ability to plan has been squandered on details. The real structure, of which the house, the school, or the monumental city hall forms a part, has come into being without a plan; or rather, the plan which lies in back of it has no intelligible relation to the practice of architecture or to the art of living well in an urban community.

IV

We have so far dealt only with the first stage of American city planning and city development; and with the effects that they continue to produce upon architecture. Up to the time of the World's Fair in 1893 the practices which we have been describing were set in the foundations of every American city, unquestioned and unvarying. At the time of the World's Fair the architects of the country banded together as a united profession. In laying out of the exposition grounds they introduced the concept of beauty and order and symmetry into the design of the miniature city; they brought together landscape architecture, building, and sculpture, and gave the ordinary man a hint of something that he was missing in the ramshackle, unstable, hit-or-miss building that characterized the growing American city.

The fine example of the World's Fair gave rise to the City Beautiful movement. We may briefly sum this up as an attempt to put a pleasing front upon the scrappy building, upon the monotonous streets and the mean houses, that characterized the larger American cities. Even the smaller towns, without the resources of the metropolis, imitated its pretensions; they called in the aid of municipal art commissions, and introduced a fountain here, a statue there, and electric light pylons everywhere.

It looked, momentarily, as if the architect were about to assume the leadership in the development of the American city. Unfortunately, the exponents of the City Beautiful were for the most part no more community planners than those who preceded them. Whereas the engineer had devoted himself to sewers and street systems alone, the architectural city planner of the old school devoted himself to parkways alone, to monumental buildings alone, or to public squares alone. If the municipal engineer had been narrow and utilitarian in his rigid city plans without regard to houses and recreation areas and general amenities, the architect was equally superficial. Moreover, the demolitions demanded for his grand avenues and places were costly beyond measure, and, when all was said and done, they did not fundamentally alter the environment in which the greater part of the population, rich and poor, were still destined to live.

A number of good things no doubt came out of this effort, like the grand park systems of Chicago and Kansas City; but the architect had not faced with sufficient realism the colossal task with which he was confronted. He accepted his proposed improvements too much at the value placed upon them by the business man; as creators of land values, as a useful element in increasing the commercial attractiveness of the city.

V

Meanwhile, the skyscraper had arisen, and the modern system of underground transit had been elaborated; and the initiative went back to the hands of the engineer. It was useless to plan monumental entrances to the city, useless to lay out great places and concourses, while the mere flow and congestion of population made a good part of it spend most of its time too far either below or above ground to take note of these excellent improvements!

The engineer, who had originally planned the American city to promote traffic, now found it necessary to magnify his traffic plans and to produce a new underground city. A subway is an underground thoroughfare. Even an underground thoroughfare should have some relation to the system of streets above it and the use to which the properties it touches are put. For the most part, however, the transit systems of our American cities were planned with only one object in view; to open up new territories at the periphery of the city and to crowd more and more people into the central district. It is by crowding at both ends that the highly elaborate enterprises of modern rapid transit can be run at a sufficient profit to attract the vast outlays of capital necessary to float them. Both of these processes increased land values; both of these processes caused congestion. The congestion at the center, aided by the narrow building lot, caused the skyscraper to arise; congestion in the dormitory districts gave rise to the old style of tenement. New rapid transit lines were introduced as "a way out"; and in turn, by concentrating more feeder lines into the central trunk, they served to increase the congestion of traffic and people. In every city where this happens the situation has become so unbearable that, as the saying is, "something must be done."

VI

At this point the expert enters with a number of palliatives. He takes the ancient system of gridiron planning for granted; at best he has ultimate intentions of intersecting the parallelograms with diagonals. Like his predecessor in the early nineteenth century, he is convinced that cities must grow without limit, and that anything which would prevent their growth, anything which would fundamentally alter the lines of growth and upset the established tissue of realty values is not to be thought of. The city planner of this school has three chief cards to play, and during the last decade or so he has been fairly successful in playing them.

One: he can widen the traffic avenues and otherwise provide further facilities for traffic by bridges, tunnels, and viaducts. He can zone the various districts of the city, on the basis of existing usage, by and with the consent, above all for the benefit, of the existing owners of property. Third: he can, up to a certain point, limit the height of buildings. By concentrating upon these three points, principally perhaps upon zoning, American city planning has passed out of the grand dreams that seemed to have been awakened by the World's Fair and has come down to brass tacks.

It is our business to inquire how far this transformation has benefited communities—or if we wish to take a narrower point of view we might ask how it has aided the architect, or how it promised to shape an environment more suitable to his practice.

First, let us consider street widening. The current method is to pay for street widening to a large extent either by assessment—which implies additional occupancy along the street itself or an increased commercial value due to the more intensive use in the immediate neighborhood, or by assessment over a whole district which shares proportionately in the benefit. The second way usually leads, it may be noted in passing, to increased density of use. Thus street widening to facilitate traffic generally increases the amount of traffic in proportion to the new width. This matter has been put very admirably in the report of the Pittsburgh Committee on City Plan, for a Major Street Plan. We take the liberty of quoting from it: "There will be an ever increasing number of vehicles entering the Triangle (central district) streets. This increase will be facilitated by the improvement of the tributary streets. Increased traffic will bring higher property values; increased property values will encourage owners to erect buildings designed to pay returns related to higher valuations; this will revive the desire for more revenue producing (business making) traffic; and this will again lead to the problem of amplifying street capacity." Here is what the commission justly calls a vicious circle. The prime requirement of this type of planning is that it must pay; its chief defect is that it pays, as a rule, all too generously.

Let us now turn to zoning. This may mean one of two things. It may mean the allocation of land to a particular use, as for instance, in the first garden city at Letchworth, a certain section was from the beginning set apart for industrial development; another for residential development; another for an agricultural belt. In our American practice, however, zoning has come to mean something essentially different; it is concerned only feebly and incidentally with the community function the land will best serve; it focuses attention mainly upon the stabilizing of the existing uses and the values that are derived from them, whether these are to be the best advantage of the community or not.

Now since zoning not only occupies the most prominent place in present day city planning, but is also the usual contact point for the architect with the subject, we must dwell a little on its principles and practice.

The initial move in the case of zoning American cities was justified on the ground that industry and business, in the course of growth and expansion, blighted residential areas or passed over and completely destroyed them. Zoning would prevent all this. The necessity for conserving residential areas was a matter of the common welfare and so it was conceived that zoning could be put into effect and enforced by the exercise of police power. What constitutes police power is, of course, rather vague, but it was conceived that zoning fell within it.

The theory of zoning was thus a very simple one. In making an application of the theory, however, the practice of zoning immediately passed beyond the matter of conserving that which would accrue to the advantage of the common welfare and proceeded to utilize the principle and the power to conserve, stabilize, and enhance property values. And it is upon the efficacy of zoning as a measure which will stabilize or enhance property values that its popularity has come to hang. Has any proposed zoning ordinance the slightest possibility of going into effect unless it is so framed that it is obvious that pecuniary gains will follow to the owners of property through its enactment?

Now, pecuniary gains seldom arise out of withdrawing land from the possibility of industrial or business use. So resort is had to the creation of many residential categories so as to provide finely graded areas

of differential exclusiveness. In this way, property values are stabilized
and enhanced. This consideration now furnishes the main ground for
the popularity of zoning.

If we turn back to the original concept it is clear that zoning as it
is now carried on can hardly be justified on the ground that, by and
large, it serves the interest of the common welfare. It may be that the
segregation of economic classes is quite the reverse. In any event,
whether the practice as developed is for good or evil, it is perfectly
evident that the constitutional ground upon which zoning was originally based has been cut away by the creation of an ever increasing
number of categories.

Let us now turn from the social to the economic and physical aspects of zoning. As generally advocated and practiced, zoning is an
admitted compromise with existing conditions in the interest of "stabilizing" values and uses. When these existing conditions are the result
of haphazard and badly related development, such stabilization may
conceivably retard one desirable, though momentarily unpleasant,
change normally brought about by economic pressure.

We may safely say that most of our present zoning lacks any degree of positive coordination with a well conceived distribution of low-
density areas permanently isolated from traffic invasion. Such isolation
would conflict with the universal expectation of rise in land value in
residential as in other districts. Zone plans are frequently accompanied
by requirements for wide streets and deep setbacks which are naively
advocated for safety in case that zoning does not work. Few seem to
appreciate the direct relation between change in character of property
and the accumulation of costs resulting from extravagant expenditures
in public improvements and wasteful areas which our system of land
development entails. Zoning under such conditions is popular because
there is so much property being adversely affected by changes resulting
from lack of regulation. It does not follow that regulation in the interest
of abating these changes is either desirable or effective.

On the other hand, from the standpoint of the architect, zoning has
imposed innumerable restrictions, many of them futile and unimpor-
tant, which tend to increase the complexity of his task in planning for
the use of property, often preventing the introduction of desirable
innovations suggested by an intelligent appreciation of his problem.
So rigid are these rules in many of our prominent zoned cities and so
little have they to do with the essential principles of community plan-

ning that a well conceived Town Planning and Housing Scheme, on the lines of the best Dutch and English precedents, would be possible only in new districts which have not yet been trimmed up by the procrustean ax of the zoning expert.

In sum, the only rational end for which zoning can exist, namely, to promote better communities for living and working and bringing up children, is actually often hindered by the present applications of zoning. Need we wonder that current city planning has so little interest for the architect?

What applies to zoning applies with slight changes to limiting the height of buildings, with which this measure is often associated. Setback rules for the upper stories and limitation of heights are provided for without any genuine attempt to relate these provisions to the development of the city as a whole. The result of these rules has lately been hailed as a triumph for architecture, because of the picturesque skyline the building often presents, even when the regulations are applied in a purely automatic fashion; but all the while the growth of skyscrapers to the permissible height more and more swamps the recognition of any particular building, and obliterates any approach that the solitary structure may have.

The present order of city planning and city regulation is concerned with what is, in every sense of the word, a transitory city. It is not unfair to say that it accepts without overt criticism the tradition which holds that a city exists solely for the purpose of commercial gain; that it looks with equanimity upon the absorption of more and more people into cities and city-regions already overcrowded; and that it has nothing to offer against the continuous process of removal and destruction caused by shifts in land values except the tentative suggestion that these values may be stabilized for a while by zoning. Through zoning, our city planners are ready to proceed against "unfair competition" in the intensive use of land. But zoning plans and height regulations and street widenings and transit maps all assume a more and more intensive use of land, a continual shift in the function and character of each area, and the steady accretion of financial values to the existing properties.

So it should not seem unnatural that housing, that civic art, that the daily requirements of recreation, apart from the Sunday auto excursion to distant park areas play minor parts in the current city planning schemes. The architect, in his capacity as community planner, is left out of consideration; while as an individual, the architect's work shares the transitory quality of the city itself. The fate of the Illinois Trust and Savings Bank in Chicago, and the Madison Square Presbyterian Church, in New York, more or less awaits all the buildings of the modern American city under present conditions. No matter how adequately designed, or how satisfying their facades, our buildings are doomed to be obliterated as land values shift and a more intensive development is found necessary, not, like Wren's city after three hundred years, but after thirty. Their only alternative fate is to be condemned, like the Boston Customs House, to a more ignominious form of preservation. Such stability of purposes and values, as has made the precincts of Piccadilly Circus serve as a gay resort and market from the time of St. James' Fair in the late Middle Ages, or has given Westminster its characteristics as a political and religious center for an even longer time, does not reside in the American city in its present state. In New York, Washington Square College might have been within walking distance of the Astor Library, had not the library moved to a site within walking distance of Columbia University—only to find Columbia University moved. These examples are typical. It is not architecture that the American city needs under the present mode of development, but scene-painting.

VII

In all this we are far from saying that the present type of city planning is without value. If a disease cannot be cured outright it is perhaps better to relieve the patient's suffering a little than to offer him no help at all. But what we desire to point out is that when our city planner sets out to correct the difficulties and evils that have resulted in the development of our growing cities, his work must remain ineffective, as long as he permits the source of these evils and difficulties to remain. So far he has made no move to touch the source. In city planning, to adopt Thoreau's well known words, there are hundreds who are trimming the branches of evil, to one who is hacking at the root. As long as the dogma that all cities must continue to grow, and that growth is desirable because it increases land values and fosters profitable public utilities like subways and profitable private investments like skyscrapers—as long as this dogma is accepted without skepticism and without reserve there is literally no end to the city planner's task, and, in any fundamental sense, *no beginning.*

VIII

Now that we have analyzed the historic practice in developing American communities, and the current methods of correcting and improving this practice, we can perhaps understand a little better why the architect has lost his leadership in the present city planning movement. The main reason is that current city planning has nothing to offer the architect. Its practices are not those that have given the architectural profession its independence, its power, its dignity, its sense of service. Our present city planning has not merely done nothing to remove the economic difficulties that hinder the architect, and that keep all our housing, even our best, at such low levels; it has not even clearly analyzed the situation and called attention to the difficulties. The plans which it lays down, the restrictions which it imposes, are for the most part a hindrance to genuine community planning, for the reason that they have been aimed only at development in the narrow, commercial sense—greater area, more people, increasing density, increasing traffic, more area, more people and more traffic, without end.

What then, is genuine community planning?

Our present city planning deals for the most part with the bare physical framework of the city. Community planning comprehends not merely the physical layout of streets, avenues, blocks, and traffic arteries, but the whole environment, including the work, the housing, the recreation, the customs and habits of the people who make up the community. Rousseau said that houses make a town, people make a city; and we may add that the combination of houses and people provide the situation for the community planner.

Now, in dealing with his individual client, the architect does not merely pay attention to his rough physical requirements, to drainage and circulation, and so forth; he also pays attention to the specific use or uses to which a building is to be put, and to the needs and interests of his client, interpreted in the broadest sense. Community planning carries this habit of mind over to the community as a whole. Just as it is impossible to design a good house if the owner wants to spend the greater part of his available capital on a garage, so it is impossible to do any effective community planning if the majority of people are more interested in making financial "values" than in creating for themselves the real goods that come from houses well-planned, recreation areas well-placed, and community buildings which serve every member to their maximum capacity. In the huge electric map that graced an official exhibition of the City of New York not long ago, the light turned proudly on from moment to moment to call attention to the police stations, the fire houses, the prisons and the hospitals that the city boasted —in short, to the whole elaborate system of preventive agents which the city as a whole supports, in lieu of the positive goods upon which a better designed community would spend the major portion of its income. In fact, the greater part of our civic "improvements" entail an outlay on remedies which should be expended in creating conditions which would avoid the necessity for such vast amounts of negative spending. Genuine community planning, therefore, seeks more to provide for a sound development in the future than it does to obliterate by direct attack all our errors and misdemeanors of the past. It does not seek superficially to remedy the inherent defects of the existing cities; it seeks to supplant them.

Community planning does not ask by what desperate means a city of 600,000 people can add another 400,000 during the next generation, nor how a city of 7 millions may enlarge its effective borders so as to include 29 million. It begins, rather, at the other end, and it asks, with Mr. Ebenezer Howard, how big must a city be to perform effectively all of its social, educational, and industrial functions. It attempts to establish minima and maxima for different kinds of communities, depending upon their character and function. If the established practices of industry, commerce, and finance tend to produce monstrous agglomerations which do not contribute to human welfare or happiness, community planning must question these established practices, since the values they create have nothing to do with the essential welfare of the community itself, and since the condition thus created is inimical to the stable, architectural development of the community. If the mind of the engineer turns naturally to the practices of so-called city planning, with their vast demands for purely engineering services such as street widening, water systems, subways, and what not, it should be equally apparent that the ideas and traditions of architecture can come to fruit only in genuine community planning, by a comprehensive attempt to attack the problem from the ground up. This effort, we do not hesitate to say, may in some cases obviate the need for the vast engineering palliatives which are currently offered as "solutions."

IX

It has not been our purpose to offer any final suggestions in this report. Our effort has been to define clearly the difference between two objectives, between city planning and community planning, between promoting commercial values and promoting primarily human values, between attempting to rectify the resultant defects of the traditional scheme of American city development, and centering upon the causes which lie at the bottom of them. Before any community can undertake to plan its future development, it must face this alternative.

The planning of communities is probably the greatest undertaking that we have before us. It is the making of the mold in which future generations will be formed. Plainly, it is not a task for one group, one profession; still less for any section of one group or one profession. Community planning is a cooperative undertaking. Its aims and its technique are of such a nature, however, that architects, because of their training and experience, should be fitted to take a leading and not a subordinate part.

The engineer thinks of human beings as weights, loads, elements to be used in production or traffic; the architect, on the other hand, looks upon buildings and cities as the makers of men, and he cannot help planning structures and towns so that they will react upon and mold the characters of the inhabitants. The business of the architect as community planner is to study the needs and aspirations of human beings—not merely in their capacity as subway-riders or "robots"—and to plan buildings which will fit them and help them to grow.

For the present, all perhaps that the architect can do is to clarify in his own mind, and in the minds of his fellow citizens, the essential difference between city planning, so-called, and community planning. We have offered the foregoing analysis with due hesitation and reserve; and our aim has been to present a basis for thought rather than to do other people's thinking. With the clarification that we believe is necessary, must come a fundamental study of the needs of our cities; more than that, a study of the human need for cities, and a determination of what elements are essential for every community, and what elements tend to undermine and endanger its existence.

In America we have never stopped growing long enough to diagnose the fundamental ailments of modern urban growth. Until we, individually and as a community, undertake this examination, the field for community planning will be limited, and the architect will continue to design, in subservience to the forces outside his work which are daily determining his milieu. Once our American communities are ready to alter, not simply their superficial physical characteristics, but some of their fundamental habits and traditions, then community planning will be possible. It is our belief that it will be to the supreme advantage of the architect to hasten this day. When it comes, his genuine opportunity for service to the community and his genuine opportunity as a creative artist, will come, too.

F. L. ACKERMAN   WILLIAM T. JOHNSON

FREDERICK BIGGER   RUDOLPH WEAVER

JOHN IRWIN BRIGHT   E. B. GILCHRIST

M. H. GOLDSTEIN   F. R. WALKER

HENRY WRIGHT   CLARENCE S. STEIN, *Chairman*

PART II

I

In the report for 1924 we approached the relation of the architect to community planning by way of history. We endeavored to show that certain conditions had arisen in the past, as a result of the hasty and scattered development of American communities, which placed obstacles in the way of any comprehensive attempt to establish an architectural, esthetic, and human relationship between the particular building upon which the architect was at work and the framework of the community. Against the traditional American practices of building up and tearing down our cities, we set the idea of community planning.

As a result of continued studies and investigations which various members of the Committee on Community Planning have made, we now feel competent to go perhaps a step further. Instead of approaching the problem of the individual building through the community, we propose to turn the situation around; we shall discuss the problem of community planning through a closer analysis of the factors that go into the individual building; the factors that condition every step of the architect's work and in the end make for good or bad design.

The elements that go to make an individual piece of architecture fall into three groups. The first set is fixed by the client; we can put them under the general head of "requirements." Here the guiding conditions are the functions that the building serves, the costs the client is willing to meet, and the level of the client's taste and culture. Except indirectly, by exerting an influence over the general level of taste, the architectural profession has no control over these factors; and for the purposes of this study we may therefore put them to one side.

The second group that enters into the design of a building consists of the architect, the building workers, the craftsmen, the artists, and the "immaterial" factor known as the state of the arts. It is within this department that important advances have been made within the last generation in America, partly through improvements in the technical education of the architect, partly through the importation of foreign craftsmen, partly through the development of architectural facilities for training building workers, and finally through the general organization of the building industry. Architecture has profited by the great scientific and industrial advances of the last century, and a great architect like Wren need no longer fear that his proudest work may come to grief through the incompleteness of his knowledge of mathematics and physics, when the necessary tables and equations for calculating loads and stresses are at the fingers' ends of subordinate workers.

Up to the present our plans for improving architectural practice have touched only these two groups. We have attempted gradually to educate the client and raise the standard of taste; and for this purpose we have had as allies a battalion of magazines devoted to better building and better homes; while an increasing output of books has at least heightened interest in the problem, even if the paths that are pointed out by the authors lead in diverse and often contrary directions. At the same time we have made certain notable advances in the organization of our own profession and of the building industry. As a result of these activities there has been real improvement on many sides.

All the while, however, we have ignored a third set of factors which underlies the other two, and which conditions every improvement we attempt to make. The neglected element is that of environment or "place": it is literally the foundation of all the architect's work, and in so far as he has ceased to reckon with it he has built upon sand. By "place" we do not merely mean site; we mean lot, street, avenue, city, region, together with all the utilities that must be connected up with a building before it functions as a living organism. Put in this broad way, "place" obviously affects cost, purpose, design, and technical equipment; and if the architect is to play a determining part in the design of a building we must deal with this element before we can deal straightforwardly with any other.

It is on this local and communal factor that the Committee on Community Planning continues to center attention, to round out the work that has already been done by the American Institute of Architects with respect to public education, to the training of the architect, and to the organization of the building trades.

II

Given an individual structure that must be erected within urban limits, how does the environment affect the architect?

The first thing that calls for note is the mere quantity of land available. Where the congestion of population is great, where land values are high, where the architect must crowd the land to the last available limit allowed under the building code, the inner purpose of the building must often be trimmed and curtailed to accord with the extraneous purpose of carrying the load of rent and taxes on a crowded site. The result is that design takes on a purely utilitarian character until, perhaps, the architect gets to the upper stories, when, if there be a zoning ordinance to curb the demand for maximum floor space, he may have a narrow opportunity to pay a little attention to the amenities of design. More than this: the prospective congestion of population and the rise of site values have a more important effect upon the durability of the building than the materials that are used. Where land values are high, moreover, the site absorbs money that should have gone into the permanent structure, and by continuous absorption (appreciation of values) keeps any building from being permanent! In greater or less degree this factor exerts a controlling interest over architecture in every large urban area.

The size and shape of the lot is the next place element. Depth, width, and shape are in large part determined by the city plan. In all our urban communities the demand for street frontage has increased the ratio of streets to buildings and has fostered, as was pointed out in the last report, the deep, narrow lot. In so far as buildings are considered solely as a means for increasing the turnover of capital this type of layout is admirable. We are gradually learning, however, that the street is a function of the building, and vice versa, so that if we have wide streets, heavily paved, and carrying a large amount of traffic, we will be driven to erect tall buildings upon them in order to meet the carrying charges; and by the same token, if we erect tall buildings we are driven to further expenditures through widening or duplicating the streets, by underground tubes or aerial avenues, and the "economy" of the tall building is to a large degree offset by the vast public expenses that must be incurred in even partially serving it. The notion that streets can be laid down without respect to use is a fallacy. Wide streets equipped with expensive utilities, prolonged into a suburban area, determine the character of its development: in many cases they make the tenement house of four or more stories all but a necessity, whereas streets planned directly for residence service would make the two-story house possible. We habitually permit the municipal engineer to give a form to the city without determining the functions; whereas *the form is meaningless and obstructive except in definite relation to the functions.* As a result of this practice a dreadful monotony prevails. One street is like another; one site is like another; and finally our cities boast miles and miles of anonymous houses and insignificant public buildings, duplicated as blindly and mechanically as the streets in which they are framed.

The city plan likewise exerts an influence over the placement and composition of buildings; it determines whether a building shall be approached or whether it shall be reached in sidelong fashion. Some of our cities which have the conventional gridiron have been trying desperately to provide civic centers for their major public buildings, where they may be grouped in a monumental way, but the system of gridiron planning creates no natural predominating sites for naturally predominating buildings; and where by accident we have an odd corner, we have so lost appreciation of site value in anything but the financial sense of the word that it as likely as not will be occupied by an indifferent structure. Moreover, our monumental interest in major civic centers neglects the fact that there are a host of lesser buildings that deserve the same treatment. The neighborhood church, the school, the community center, yes, the moving picture house could be planned with much more felicity if they had sites that dominated the neighborhood. In this way the church, perhaps, might avoid the gratuitous steeple, and spend the money saved thereby on finer interior sculpture and painting; or, to take an example from the opposite end of the scale, the moving picture theatre might dispense with its cumbrous and ugly marquee, spattered with lights, and still sufficiently attract the attention of the passing neighbors. More adequately than by the mere exclusion practiced in zoning regulations, definite areas might be set aside for the grouping of garages; and there would be other definite areas, definitely related, for parking space. Besides giving accessibility and good position to certain buildings, an adequate plan would give privacy and isolation to hospitals and schools, placing them apart from the noise, odor, and dust of the traffic arteries. It is impossible for individuals and institutions to provide adequate sites for themselves when a whole tract is indiscriminately cut into blocks of equal length and identical shape, each parcel of which is sold recklessly to the highest bidder, as opportunity offers; and no skill of the architect or engineer will ever overcome the inadequacy of unsuitable lot shapes, bad frontages, and antagonistic neighbors.

Our lack of community planning along these roughly outlined paths has unfortunate esthetic results; and these must be emphasized. The architect is often driven to give a false individual stress to a building whose sole emphasis should come from its position in the community plan; this condition has fostered mere idiosyncrasy and showing off, and has kept the architect from expressing the general spirit of neighborliness which would bring together and give a certain harmony to modern buildings as surely as it did to the varied structures of eighteenth century Boston or Philadelphia. The little island on which the old State House at Boston stood was quite enough to establish its position; it could remain a small building and still be important and interesting. A good community plan is one that enables the architect to take advantage of the support of surrounding buildings, in carrying out his composition, instead of trying to shout them down and draw attention away from them.

But it is not merely the lot and the block layout and the city plan that affect the character of the architect's work; he is directly influenced again and again by apparently remoter elements. The character of the city itself, its rate of growth, the stability of its use-zones (if it has established any), are all conditioned by its relation to industry, credit, power, transportation, and regional resources. It is important that the architect should realize here what factors are working to his advantage and what factors are working against him. He must determine whether to work for congestion or decentralization; whether to remain content with the narrower and narrower limits that are imposed on him, or whether he shall endeavor to promote a fresh start. He must decide whether he is prepared to take the lead in community planning, or whether he will be content to be perpetually frustrated and balked, even in his purely esthetic conceptions, by the framework that has been so rigorously prepared for him. In sum, he must decide whether cities and buildings exist in order to enable people to live more complete and beautiful lives, or whether he believes that people exist in order to increase the financial value of our stony cage of streets and buildings.

Assuming that the architect sees the necessity of reacting upon and humanizing our present environment, we will now examine in detail the points where community planning is prepared to challenge our existing methods of planning and building. Our thesis is that architecture and community planning are inseparable. It is only on paper that buildings exist by themselves, and it is only on paper that they can achieve an esthetic triumph without respect to their placement, their neighbors, their approach. The great mass of our buildings today, if not unsightly, are unsitely; and that is because the architect has not had the opportunity to exercise the necessary correlative function of community planning.

III

In order to simplify our analysis we shall confine attention at first to the relation of the dwelling house to the community plan. Here we can restrict ourselves to definite factors of cost in relation to use, and we have the opportunity to compare similar projects with similar requirements in different parts of the country. What applies to the dwelling house applies with certain changes to other types of building, and other kinds of community layout.

In reckoning the cost of houses we have hitherto centered attention almost entirely upon the house itself and the land. We have, therefore, uncritically assumed that low land values, low labor charges, and low costs of materials were the great desiderata in building economically. From a series of studies that Mr. Henry Wright has made during the last five years, it has become apparent that we have been barking up the wrong tree. Putting together a number of examples from various parts of the country, it becomes apparent that in the finished product not more than 55 per cent to 60 per cent is represented in the finished structure itself. The remaining portion covers a multitude of accessory matters, in which public improvement costs, utility connections, carrying charges, and so forth represent the major part.

At the present time the architect generally touches only 55 per cent of the cost of a house. One of the outstanding elements in cost is outside the province of both the architect and the community planner; namely, the rate of money. Yet the New York Housing and Regional Planning Commission has found in dealing with the problem of rebuilding the obsolete tenements that a 1 per cent drop in the interest rate produces as great a result in the cost reduction as a 15 per cent saving of building costs on the entire structure. No other factor is as important in fixing the cost of housing as payment for the use of money.

When one starts with the community as a whole instead of the individual buyer of land or owner, it is possible to make a great improvement in plot planning. This does not mean that it is necessary to do away with individual ownership; it means only that the size and shape of the individual plot should be determined by the best needs of the whole. Instead of fitting our houses to plots whose size and shape were determined purely on commercial grounds, community planning demands that the commercial arrangements shall be shaped to best serve the character of the whole development. Let us make this clear by a concrete example.

In Plate 1,* original plan, we have a tract which was planned as a whole; and except for slight variations in the curved roads, the lots consist of identical rectangles; for all practical purposes we have the typical gridiron treatment. In Study No. 1 we have a diagrammatic scheme with a good part of the unnecessary streets eliminated. Finally, in Study No. 2 the tract is completely replotted in such a way as to give to each of the houses not merely a backyard but an interior park. None of the differences in plot size under the second treatment are great enough to interfere with the ordinary terms of sale; but by making them the planner has escaped from a monotonous method of platting.

The next step consists in carrying this economy through the house itself. The individual detached or semi-detached house that is common

* Not reprinted in this volume.

in our American cities in all their more recent portions gives neither privacy nor comfort nor free exposure to air and sunlight; just the contrary. By combining houses in units of six and eight, as was done in the War housing experiments of the United States Housing Corporation and the United States Shipping Board, a unit that lends itself to more adequate architectural treatment is provided, wasted land is redeemed, and a greater degree of privacy is assured. The gridiron plan with its automatic block subdivision eliminates the architect: if one site is like another and one house like another a standardized plan will meet every emergency. Once the automatic subdivision is thrown in the scrap-heap, the work of the architect becomes a necessity, for in setting down a functional subdivision the design and plan of the house will vary with its immediate site and purpose; and there is no limit to the variety and interest of house grouping that the architect may practice. Plates 2 and 3, which represent studies both in single family houses and apartments made at different times by members of the committee, give a rough indication of the effects of correlating house planning and community planning. Proportion and accent and relationship to natural features such as trees, hedges, and gardens may here take the place of Romantic styles, Tudor, Georgian, Spanish and what not, that now arise in distracting medley in the best of our suburbs. In this domain economy and beauty walk hand in hand. Both of them work for the general interest of the community.

We carry the process of community planning a step farther, and go on to redeem a little more of our extravagant "waste-land" to the uses of architectural beauty. The possibilities of achieving greater interest and important economies through planning streets and utilities in connection with the actual designs for buildings are so huge that, for anyone who has not gone exhaustively into the matter, they must at first seem incredible. Again we go back for illustration to the two layouts we have just compared. The total number of lots is the same; the area of the lots has increased a little through better planning; but at the same time the amount of space devoted entirely to streets and alleys has been almost cut in half. The land thus saved has more than doubled the amount of space for parks and playgrounds and gardens. This is not merely a saving of space. Turn for even more remarkable demonstration to Plate 4. The first plan shows an actual tract at the border of New York City, as automatically laid out by the municipal engineer's office and as dedicated by the realtor to sale and turnover. The second plan shows the same tract replatted for the purpose of living. Not merely have great advances been made in gaining special sites for markets, industries, and community buildings, but in this new plan enough money has been saved in reducing the amount of *unnecessary* streets and public utilities to *cover the cost of purchasing the land in the entire tract*. The unnecessary streets of our automatic development are not only a first burden; they remain a continuous burden on the community, and preempt for their own upkeeping and interest-charges funds which should be devoted to public amenities. Community planning in this department effects a double economy.

Here are the major economies that community planning makes possible. As a body, architects have scarcely begun to appreciate that the cost of the external accessories of a building, accessories which in themselves contribute nothing by their extravagance to the comfort of the occupants, amount to a very large percentage of the total cost. To put it briefly: we splurge on public utilities, and we skimp on art. And all the while we do this the more perfect application of art, the union of architecture and community planning, would balance up our expenditures and make better utilities and better art both possible. When we drag our site and utilities costs ruthlessly into the open, we find that they are sapping the very life-blood out of our building. How long will we go on diverting to extravagantly conceived streets, surfaces, pavements, junctions, curbs, sidewalks, street and lateral sewers, disposal tanks, separate storm water drains, water, gas and electrical systems, funds that might go into more interesting and spirited touches in our houses and public buildings and our whole communal environment? On our answer to this question the fitness and beauty of the great mass of buildings that we will continue to put up depends.

IV

It should be plain from these considerations that the next great architectural advance will consist in redeeming to architecture the control over the place and site factors; that is to say, the undertaking of community planning and architecture as part and parcel of one process. This control was exercised by the architect in the past in the laying out of the aristocratic quarters of Edinburgh, London, and Bath in the eighteenth century; and we shall have to recover it and exercise it on a wider scale, for the benefit of the whole community, if our present gains in skill and taste and organization are not to be nullified by factors that at present lie beyond the architect's control.

As long as congestion, high site values, and rapid turnover are the aims of urban building, there is little chance of the architect's being able to practice his art with any prospect of stable achievement within our existing centers. Within our growing cities he is hampered by a fine network of established usages, vested interests, high land values, and reckless city plans and city improvements, to say nothing of the procrustean set of regulations designed to reduce the sanitary hazards of bad planning and human hazards of fire. In these centers the architect is handicapped both by bad conditions and by regulations which are established to combat them; and sometimes it is hard to say which is worse, for within the greater part of our zoned and platted cities the finer type of development which the architect and community planner has worked out is frequently prohibited by law!

Does this mean then that nothing can be done? On the contrary. The continued increase of population, the continued demand for new buildings, homes, offices, schools, factories, means that there is an infinite opportunity for the architect to exert control over the factors that have hitherto balked him, once he and his clients begin to turn their backs upon the existing centers and prepare to start with a clean slate. Our fresh increments of population may either be added automatically to existing centers, or they may be spotted in new centers. Inertia tends to produce the first development; and our business system, with its eye to turnover and prospective inflation of values, tends to further it. Intelligence and imagination, however, work in the direction of the second development; and far-sighted industrialists like Ford and Filene and Dennison, as well as a large number of industries that put the welfare of their workers on a par with the efficient location of their plant, have here and there begun to favor it. New centers, planned for a complete community life, are called "Garden Cities" in England; and it is no accident that some of the freshest and most vigorous work in house design and public building has come from the English Garden Cities, Letchworth and Welwyn, and the Dutch garden suburbs, like Hilversum. The architect has nothing to gain from the forces of inertia, the forces that are heaping up and making more intolerable our big cities, for in the long run these forces will dispense with his services. He has everything to gain from the comprehensive and enlightened group action necessary to create the Garden City, and to create that new regional framework, based upon the more effective relation of communities and industries to the natural environment, to power, to water, to fresh air and "nature," in which Garden Cities will be possible.

We cannot in the present report go into all the possibilities that await architecture when we are able to effect a change in venue, to enable architecture and community planning to proceed hand in hand. It is enough to say that when community interests take precedence over business values, along the lines already laid down in the treatment of house and neighborhood planning, similar economies are possible for the city and region as a whole. It is in the planning and construction of new communities, rather than in the constricted shell of the old, that the architect will have the opportunity to prove his metal and demonstrate the full measure of his abilities. Instead of congratulating ourselves upon our undoubted achievements, despite the handicaps that have been laid upon us, let us prepare to remove the handicaps. By doing this, architecture will not continue to bloom merely in the crevices unoccupied by business; it will spread over the entire field of American life, and, in Professor Lethaby's fine words, will create "form in civilization."

F. L. ACKERMAN	EUGENE HENRY KLABER
FREDERICK BIGGER	WM. SCHUCHARDT
JOHN IRWIN BRIGHT	RUDOLPH WEAVER
E. B. GILCHRIST	C. M. WINSLOW
M. H. GOLDSTEIN	HENRY WRIGHT
WM. T. JOHNSON	CLARENCE S. STEIN, *Chairman*

Suggested Readings

PART ONE: CONSERVATION AND COMMUNITY

Hays, Samuel P., *Conservation and the Gospel of Efficiency: The Progressive Conservation Movement.* Cambridge, Mass.: Harvard University Press, 1959.

Powell, John W., *Report on the Lands of the Arid Region of the United States, With a More Detailed Account of the Lands of Utah.* Washington, D.C., 1878.

Stegner, Wallace, *Beyond the Hundredth Meridian: John Wesley Powell and the Second Opening of the West.* Boston: Sentry, 1962.

PART TWO: LANDSCAPE ARCHITECTURE AND PARK PLANNING

Cleveland, H. W. S., *Landscape Architecture as Applied to the Wants of the West.* Pittsburgh: University of Pittsburgh Press, 1965. Originally published 1873.

Downing, Andrew Jackson, *Rural Essays.* New York, 1853.

Mumford, Lewis, "The Renewal of the Landscape," in *The Brown Decades: A Study of the Arts of America, 1865-1895.* New York: Dover Publications, Inc., 1955.

Olmsted, Frederick Law, Jr., and Theodora Kimball, eds., *Frederick Law Olmsted, Landscape Architect, 1822-1903.* New York: G. P. Putnam's Sons, 1922, 2 Vols.

Reps, John W., "Cemeteries, Parks, and Suburbs: Picturesque Planning in the Romantic Style," in *The Making of Urban America: A History of City Planning in the United States*. Princeton, N.J.: Princeton University Press, 1965, Chap. 12.

PART THREE: HOUSING REFORM: RESTRICTIVE LEGISLATION

De Forest, Robert W., and Lawrence Veiller, eds., *The Tenement House Problem: Including the Report of the New York State Tenement House Commission of 1900*. New York, 1903, 2 Vols.

Lubove, Roy, *The Progressives and the Slums: Tenement House Reform in New York City, 1890-1917*. Pittsburgh: University of Pittsburgh Press, 1962.

————, "I. N. Phelps Stokes: Tenement Architect, Economist, Planner," *Journal of the Society of Architectural Historians*, **23** (May, 1964), 75-87.

Riis, Jacob A., *How the Other Half Lives*. New York: Sagamore Press, 1957. Originally published 1890.

————, *The Battle with the Slum*. New York, 1901.

————, *The Making of an American*. New York: Torchbook, Harper & Row, Publishers, 1966. Originally published 1903.

Warner, Sam B., Jr., *Streetcar Suburbs: The Process of Growth in Boston, 1870-1900*. Cambridge, Mass.: Harvard University Press, 1962.

PART FOUR: THE CITY BEAUTIFUL

Burnham, Daniel H., and Edward H. Bennett, *Plan of Chicago* (Prepared under the direction of the Commercial Club during the years 1906, 1907, and 1908).

Mumford, Lewis, "The Imperial Facade," in *Sticks and Stones: A Study of American Architecture and Civilization* (2nd ed.). New York: Dover Publications, Inc., 1955. Originally published 1924.

Reps, John W., "Chicago Fair and Capital City: The Rebirth of American Urban Planning," in *The Making of Urban America: A History of City Planning in the United States*. Princeton, N.J.: Princeton University Press, 1965, Chap. 18.

Wilson, William H., *The City Beautiful Movement in Kansas City*. Columbia, Mo.: University of Missouri Press, 1964.

PART FIVE: THE GARDEN CITY

Culpin, E. G., *The Garden City Movement Up-to-Date*. London: The Garden City and Town Planning Association, 1912.

Howard, Ebenezer, *Garden Cities of To-morrow*. London, 1902. Originally published 1898 as *To-morrow: A Peaceful Path to Reform*.

Mumford, Lewis, *The Culture of Cities*. New York: Harcourt, Brace & World, Inc., 1938.

Osborn, Sir Frederic, and Arnold Whittick, *The New Towns: The Answer to Megalopolis*. New York: McGraw-Hill Book Company, 1963.

Rodwin, Lloyd, *The British New Towns Policy: Problems and Implications*. Cambridge, Mass.: Harvard University Press, 1956.

Taylor, Graham R., *Satellite Cities: A Study of Industrial Suburbs*. New York: Appleton-Century-Crofts, 1915.

PART SIX: THE EMERGENCE OF PROFESSIONAL PLANNING

Adams, Frederick J., and Gerald Hodge, "City Planning Instruction in the United States," *Journal of the American Institute of Planners*, **31** (February, 1965), 43-51.

Hancock, John, "John Nolen: The Background of a Pioneer Planner," *Journal of the American Institute of Planners*, **26** (November, 1960), 302-12.

Johnson, Norman J., "A Preface to the Institute," *Journal of the American Institute of Planners*, **31** (August, 1965), 198-209.

Marsh, Benjamin C., *An Introduction to City Planning: Democracy's Challenge to the American City*. Privately printed, 1909.

Nolen, John, *New Ideals in the Planning of Cities, Towns and Villages*. New York: American City Bureau, 1919.

PART SEVEN: CONSTRUCTIVE HOUSING LEGISLATION

Lubove, Roy, "Homes and a 'Few Well-Placed Fruit Trees': An Object Lesson in Federal Housing," *Social Research*, **27** (Winter, 1960), 469-86.

Pink, Louis H., *A New Day in Housing*. New York: The John Day Company, Inc., 1928.

Wood, Edith Elmer, *The Housing of the Unskilled Wage-Earner: America's Next Problem*. New York: The Macmillan Company, 1919.

_____, *Recent Trends in American Housing*. New York: The Macmillan Company, 1931.

PART EIGHT: COMMUNITY PLANNING: THE REGIONAL PLANNING ASSOCIATION OF AMERICA

Churchill, Henry, "Henry Wright: 1878-1936," *Journal of the American Institute of Planners*, **26** (November, 1960), 293-301.

Lubove, Roy, *Community Planning in the 1920's: The Contribution of the Regional Planning Association of America*. Pittsburgh: University of Pittsburgh Press, 1963.

MacKaye, Benton, *The New Exploration: A Philosophy of Regional Planning*. Urbana, Ill.: University of Illinois Press, 1962. Originally published 1928.

New York State Commission of Housing and Regional Planning, *Report* (1926).

"Regional Plan Number," *Survey Graphic*, **54** (May 1, 1925).

Stein, Clarence S., *Toward New Towns for America*. New York: Reinhold Publishing Corp., 1957.